# UNMASKED

ISBN- 9781798188194

## C.L.Lethbridge

# DEDICATION

This book is dedicated to my two amazing loving children and my supportive family.
Especially my Dad, who has given me endless encouragement and practical help with the editing of my book.

Let it be a guide to educate my children, future generations and our loved ones of the common indicators and dynamics within toxic relationships, by making conscious decisions and choices to not go in blind as I did.

To all you amazing survivors out there, propel yourself from *surviving* to *thriving*!

Know your worth and keep shining your beautiful bright light from within.

**Love to all**

# UNMASKED

## Table of Contents:

# Introduction-

Your empowering journey starts right now. I know at this moment in time you may be feeling worthless, beaten down and hopeless after all the Narcissistic abuse you have been through; but by you being here it is the first step towards your healing and recovery.

You have broken the spell and you are now aware that all is not what it seemed- Not by a long shot.

The term "Narcissist" is casually referred to nowadays and widely thrown around to label anyone who may offend us. Society seems to have jumped on this notion, of throwing around the term when going through a break up or dealing with a difficult person.

There is such a thing as healthy narcissism when we have a balance of confidence, vanity and self-esteem.

We are not out to maliciously hurt or use others and we have insight and empathy as well as remorse and a conscience.

However, you and I both know the reason why you are reading this book, as what you have been through or still going through is anything but average and normal.

A true Narcissist with NPD has a pathological condition, which can destroy workplaces, families, relationships and individual lives.

Hidden behind closed doors all sorts of physical and emotional abuse occur at the hands of spouses, partners, parents and friends etc.

To the outside world these abusers may outwardly portray themselves as a good citizen, a hard worker, a kind neighbour, a generous spouse or a caring parent.

Unfortunately, what you see isn't always what you get.

There are many individuals out there who have the unfortunate condition called Narcissistic Personality Disorder (NPD) also known as split personality, where the individual has two or more fake personas.

There can be other overlapping and similar disorders such as antisocial disorder, borderlines, sociopathy and psychopathy etc.

My own experience is dealing with two individuals having Narcissistic Personality Disorder. The condition can affect both males and females, although statistically it affects men higher than woman.

In my book, I will be concentrating and educating you specifically about dealing with Narcissists in intimate and romantic relationships, which is reflected from my own personal accounts with these disturbed individuals.

I have survived and reached a higher level of awareness, peace and freedom and you can too; so read on, take back your power and transform your life!

# Chapter 1

## First Encounter-

The first time you meet the Narcissist they are very charming, charismatic and intriguing. You may experience an instant physical attraction. Feeling an intense spark of chemistry with this unknown stranger, which makes them even more alluring.

You feel drawn to them like magnets. The magnetic field is invisible to the naked eye but you both feel the electric force of strong attraction pulling you together. You go in blind, throwing caution to the wind and feel excited and hopeful. They are ready and waiting to morph into your ideal man or woman. They are all fake smiles and mimic your tastes, interests, hobbies even your likes and dislikes. They mirror your every move, noddingly agree with your opinions and stories thus putting you at ease. Slowly trying to share a bond and common values to gain your trust. When in reality they are observing and evaluating you, picking up and storing information on your insecurities, your weaknesses and strengths. You can't believe your luck that you have so much in common with both of you so similar fitting together like a glove. They may also play the pity card that their exes were so mean and horrible, lying and cheating on the poor Narcissist and are so happy their crazy ex is now out of their lives and they have now found you. Vocalising that they haven't laughed this much or been this happy in such a long time and that's all thanks to you. This automatically makes you feel special and you start to let your guard down. They have a sinister motive and bad intentions, so to hide their true agenda they know and say all the right words to lure you into a false sense of security. The flowing compliments and attentiveness is irresistible to you.

This fake persona the Narcissist has created is completely superficial. You think this is a process leading to the start of a blossoming romance and a potential meaningful relationship. About how two strangers open themselves up to learn about one another, finding common ground and whether they're compatible or not. Unfortunately this relies only on the victim's part as the abuser has other ideas and is busy calculating their next move.

He/she wants to consume you, possess your attention, love and ultimately control you. It is the complete opposite of a reciprocative union.
Always remember *Intensity* is not the same as *Intimacy*.
Narcissists, in some ways, are carbon copies and follow the same predictable patterns, treating you to the same cycles of abuse as anyone before you or after you will endure.

In my next chapter I explain the three stages/cycles of Narcissistic abuse starting from **Idealisation, Devaluation** and finally ending in your **Discard.**

# Chapter 2

# Idealisation-

In the beginning, you were on cloud nine experiencing love, affection, validation, generosity, maybe even kindness, understanding and support.

You were placed on a pedestal by your abuser and mirrored back to him/her all of their hopes and dreams.

At last you finally think to yourself that you have found your 'soul mate', the one who you have been waiting for.

Unfortunately, at this point you are unaware that your charming prince/princess is not who they portray themselves to be.

For if you knew the true person behind the mask at this stage, you would never willingly agree to what abuse lies ahead of you.

Abusers are well aware of this and therefore understand intellectually and instinctively that most human beings want love and security.

They will groom you like a paedophile grooms their victims and will make you feel that they can't live without you; you are their everything in the beginning.

This ensnarement is also known as 'love bombing' and is a big part of the first stage of idealisation. This is where they overvalue you and give you a place in their script of being important, flawless, perfect and can do no wrong (for now).

Unfortunately, from the dizzying heights of what goes up must come crashing down and it is only a matter of time before you have a rude awakening.

The first Narcissist, I unknowingly met when I was only 17 years old, he was aged 24, an adult. I was young, pretty, smart, fun and had a happy upbringing with my whole future ahead of me. He came into my life and swept me off of my feet, treating me like a valuable rare diamond, his irresistible Queen.

Excessive attention, flattery, flowers, gifts, trips, compliments and love letters of his undying love for me- made me feel very special and unique, overwhelmingly wanted and needed.

After only three months of knowing each other he proposed marriage to me and also possessively and obsessively got my name tattooed on his body. At the time, I thought he was demonstrating his true love and affection for me. I had no idea that it was something much more dark and sinister.

Then slowly over time I fell from grace. This was always inevitable as I was a human with real feelings, thoughts, emotions and ideas – and of course being human means having flaws, insecurities and not being perfect.

The Narcissist, from day one, had only seen me as an object of his desire, to use and control for his own agenda. I was never anything more than an accessory, an appliance who worked pretty well most of the time, but sometimes my batteries would run out or I broke down and became faulty just like a kitchen kettle or toaster might.

In turn, this made me useless to the Narcissist. A let down, an inconvenience and a big disappointment to him.

I was solely there as a mirror to reflect the Narcissist back to himself the admiration, affection and validation that they so desperately seek, but after a while the mirror starts to crack.

After a couple of weeks, months or in some cases a year or so the abuser starts to feel the empty hole, which has plagued them all of their life.

Everything they do is to try to stop and bury this horrible dreaded, dark empty feeling in their psyches.

Once your love and affection starts to wain and level out, the Narcissist feels that what they have been trying to avoid, run away from the entire time – it starts to resurface.

Instead of self-reflecting and looking deep into their inner core of why they are so unhappy and empty, they turn around and blame you for the return of their inner turmoil.

It is far too painful for a Narcissist to acknowledge or accept that it is indeed themselves who are faulty, broken and damaged. Therefore, they begin to panic trying to regain some control, turn the tables around and project their worst inner demons onto you, their partner.

He/she now has to convince themselves that you must be the problem, you always were the problem but they've only just realised you weren't so special after all, because if you were then they wouldn't have the dark feelings start to erupt back up from their depths of despair.

They would annihilate, combust everything they've known and falsely composed will disintegrate and collapse if they looked within.

Their whole fake persona – the well constructed mask will die.

They have spent their entire lives perfecting their outwardly persona and performances. They are the greatest actors, gods in their own delusional self created, play – and they will do everything in their power not to let the world know their true hideous self.

Even though you were never told the rules, you were I'm afraid playing a game. A game that you never knew about or could ever imagine, a game where whatever you do or say you will always lose.

A game where you are the pawn to be moved, maneuvered and manipulated in anyway the Narcissist sees fit. After all you should be privileged that you were chosen to serve the Narcissist his every whim.

Don't you know that they are superior and god-like compared to us mere mortals?

You are only there as a distraction, a servant, an object to be used and abused for only the Narcissist's gain.

They are self-absorbed, self-centred, arrogant and always feel entitled. You and your well-being are of no concern. If you don't comply with or question the Narcissist then you will be put back in your place and encounter the next stage where devaluation begins..........

# Chapter 3

# Devaluation-

Everything you used to say or do now annoys and irritates the Narcissist – you feel like you are walking on eggshells, desperate to regain some balance and warmth which you lapped up in the beginning. This may start off very subtlety as if being drip fed to you or it could appear suddenly and unexpectedly.

You are confused and bewildered, where has he/she gone you constantly ask yourself?

They will blow hot/cold and do a push and pull dance to keep you off balance and in a state of heightened anxiety and doubt.

They start to criticise what you look like, your clothes, your hobbies, your friends and everything they pretended to like in the beginning. They will put you down and either make overt or covert comments designed to provoke you – make you feel worthless and 'not enough' any more. They may rage at you and spew all their inner verbal turmoil on to you, sit back and watch you wallow and wither in distress.

Then once they start to feel a bit better after knocking you down a peg or two, they will act like nothing has happened and revert back to the original charming mask.

Very soon your treatment will get worse and worse. You will constantly be dragged back and forth into the two different worlds of his/her split personality. Thrown in now will be doses of affection balanced by unpredictable bouts of stonewalling and the cruel silent treatment.

The purpose of this is to punish you for disobeying or maybe criticising the Narcissist, whether it is real or perceived.

Having experienced this first-hand, I found the silent treatment one of the worst kinds of abuse. It is deliberate and insidious, meant to cause great pain and displeasure. It makes you feel small, insignificant and is designed to make you feel worthless as if you don't exist anymore; you are dead to the Narcissist!

It is very eerie to watch how they can switch from mask to mask so easily, often transforming into icey robotic, lifeless beings. They are emotionless and cold blooded like a reptile oozing callousness and indifference.

The atmosphere is horrendous with subzero temperatures.

Naturally you begin to interact with your abuser by trying to understand what is happening, begging for some type of acknowledgement and communication.

Many survivors would rather the rages and screaming, even recieving physical abuse as this at least makes them feel visible and alive in their abuser's eyes.

Being cut off without any interaction is mind blowing. We are all social creatures and it feels especially cruel when these are the people we love and care about who can be so inhuman, unloving, eerily calm and sadistic.

The truth is at this point while your head is spinning and maybe you're crying, screaming trying to get your abuser to listen and acknowledge you – the more powerful they feel.

They get a massive hit of superiority and gratification watching you fall apart right in front of them, knowing that they are the reason for your hurt and pain.

It makes them feel invincible and gives them a high drug experience of opulence and grandeur. It reinforces their false self that after all they were right, if they can push your buttons and get you to react emotionally then they are in fact god-like.

A higher superior being who feels powerful and in control. They are the puppeteers and you are their puppet.

They own you, possess you and ultimately control you.

It is during the devaluation stage that a Narcissist doesn't care whether they are gaining positive or negative feelings from you.

All they care about is inflicting an emotional reaction, whether good or bad. It makes no difference to them, as long as you are reacting to their beat and playing their game.

You are still supplying them energy either way.

By now they are so bored anyway of the positive repetitive chatter from you, that they now want to spice it up a bit and push your boundaries watching you fall to pieces for their satisfaction.

They love to constantly create drama and chaos as they are perpetually bored.

Your novelty and the brand new, shiny feeling that they felt in the beginning has worn off and now grates on the Narcissist's nerves.

Once finished being toyed and played with you will soon be thrown away, just like a new toy that a child gets bored with before they move onto the next best thing.

During my time with my Narcissist, I married and spent 16 years in these conflicting states of mind games.

I went back and forth between the two cycles of re-idealisation and devalue, back and forth, trapped on the rollercoaster of emotions.

After being devalued at times and when my Narcissist knew I had had enough, and he could sense me pulling away or starting to stand up for myself, he would then go back to the future faking, the charming guy who I fell in love with.

Dragging me back into his bottomless abyss, pulling me deeper and deeper into soul crushing torture and the more I had invested in the relationship the longer I stayed, powerless and helpless drifting in and out of reality.

After he treated me like crap he would get down on his hands and knees and would beg me not to leave him. Playing with my heartstrings, crying crocodile tears if need be, insincere fake apologies, promising to change and be the person I wanted so deeply.

I was hooked back in and the cycles continued throughout the 16 years. Once I had children the abuse escalated as my Narcissist new then, that I was fully in it for the long haul and wasn't going anywhere – for I was now completely and utterly dependent on him. Emotionally, mentally, physically, financially and psychologically. I was now officially stuck and trapped in a cat and mouse game where I would be toyed with, manipulated, cheated on, lied to, physically assaulted, blamed and all my great expectations in the beginning managed down and eroded.

Throughout these overlapping cycles you will experience what is called 'cognitive dissonance'.

Our minds become so confused by the abuse and performances from the constant switch of masks. This results in these conflicting thoughts and leads us to a mindset of not trusting our own perception of reality.

It happens when these contradicting thoughts continue to fight each other, going back and forth resulting in a constant state of anxious confusion and continuous battling of disorientation between the two beliefs.

In the end, I felt so worn down and emotionally battered and bruised I didn't know for certain, what was my true reality. The one the Narcissist falsely manufactured or the truth – the real one I was seeing, feeling and experiencing?

I trusted the Narcissist more than I trusted myself, I spent half my life with this person. I doubted and ignored my deep inner self and the truth, as the reality was far too painful and devastating to admit.

I felt like I had no choice but to accept what the abuser had created, designed, portrayed and continually told me. On top of that I waited, always hoping and anticipating for the first mask in the beginning to reappear.

Throughout my relationship I saw glimpses of that false mask which again kept me locked in a confused state. Imagining and wishing that my life would return finally back to the love and affection that I had received in the initial stage.

Never in my wildest dreams (nightmares) could I have anticipated that the original mask was an illusion, a ploy to con me into entering an invisible sinister contract with masquerader.

All along he was a con artist, an impostor in order to disguise his true underlying evil intentions. I spent 16 years minimising, rationalising, and excusing his continuous bad behaviour, burying my head deeper into the sinking sand– I was in constant denial.

It is at this point where if you are still struggling with these conflicting beliefs the only way to move forward and gain clarity is to except that the man/woman that you met and fell in love with never existed.

I understand it is a painful realisation but you must become aware and accept this ultimate truth. I'm sad to say the Narcissist never loved you, only used you for the sole purpose of getting their selfish Narcissistic supply.

I know your feelings and emotions were genuine and your unconditional love for this person was real, but unfortunately it was only on your part.

Narcissists are incapable of giving love, the closest they ever get to it is feeling what we call infatuation, which they only experience in the idealisation stage where they have big hopes and expectations that this time you will be the one to fix them and make all their inner pain disappear.

For a short period of time it is plastered over, temporary concealed, a band aid – until the inevitable happens........

# Chapter 4

# The Discard -

After being dragged through the devaluation stage what is unavoidable is the following step of being horrifically discarded by your abuser.

This was always going to happen, whether you get there first and end the crazy making- or your abuser throws you away as you're no longer useful or desirable to them any more.

Your time is up, you need to be dumped on the scrap heap with all the other broken appliances who endured the same fate before you. The Narcissist is so indifferent, callous at this point and is open now for you to see his/her true colours with the mask completely ripped off. As they have no more use for you, they don't care if you see their true ugly hideous self. You have already seen glimpses of it anyway in the devaluation stage when their mask was hanging on by a thread and slipping at times.

This is the real monster behind the mask. A robotic creature who couldn't care less about your horrific realisation of who they really are. The contempt and disregard for you becomes crystal clear, even with your rose coloured glasses on you cannot deny it any more.

It is glaringly obvious and shocking to see how easy it is for the Narcissist to pull away, withdraw and detach acting like you're a complete stranger in front of them.

All those memories and experiences you felt and held dear meant absolutely nothing to your abuser. They don't care about your history or loyalty or reminisce over the good times. There is no acknowledgement or recollection of the enjoyable past events you jointly shared. No reflection of being nostalgic about the great experiences or ventures you two encountered. You only ever were their prey and once they have devoured and drained you dry your now worthless to them. Just an inconvenience, a troublesome difficult nuisance of an object, who is nothing more now than a burden.

So, now is the really fun part for the Narcissist to abandon you in the most horrific and humiliating way possible. Condemning you by ceasing to acknowledge your presence and treating you with disregard, disposing you like an empty crisp packet past its sell by date. They turn their back on everything you had built together, all the empty promises and lies come to light. They will deliberately choose to dispose of you when you're at your weakest, most vulnerable and will do so in the most cruel, cold blooded and ruthless way possible.
It is the end of their production play and now is the finale where they get to cut you out of their make-believe script. Push you off the stage, hang you by the pulley

rope that was used to change the scenery and finally erase you from their set.

This is your execution, where the guillotine goes down without a backward glance from your abuser. You signed an invisible contract that you were never aware of.
The final curtain is drawn after your unknown previous letdown performances. For you auditioned blindly, unwittingly and were cast unconsciously into a warped stage production you never suspected or knew existed.

The Narcissist inside is buzzing, ecstatic and applauding himself enthusiastically for his great orchestrated masterpiece. His choreography and engineering of the whole facade has paid off and he/she is overwhelmingly euphoric. Feeling highly charged, influential, powerful and potent.
While, your feelings are polar opposite, experiencing shock, horror, defective worthlessness and utter incomprehension of the situation you are now faced with. Never before being so bewildered and perplexed in a confused state trying desperately to gain some clarity and normality.

The initial shock is distressing and hits you like a tornado. You cannot comprehend the cruelness and ice coldness which is now your permanent reality. You are beyond devastated and traumatised by the sudden abrupt evil treatment by your abuser.

To add insult to injury and to smear more salt in your open wounds they deliver a little bit more gaslighting and blame shifting thrown in for good measure. An extra kick in the teeth, they downplay everything you thought existed, making you feel insignificant and crazy.

They undermine the whole relationship and make out people break up all the time, it's no big deal, why are you so upset?

This is why I'm leaving you, because you always overreact, over analyse everything, you're over sensitive and overdramatic all the time.

When really you are acting and responding in the most normal and humane way that any healthy human being would. Remember they are abnormal, distorting reality and taking no blame. By them twisting the whole situation around they get away without taking any accountability or responsibility and you are left being blamed and ridiculed for the bad treatment you brought on yourself – or so they want you to believe.

They casually walk away leaving you in ruins, in a heap crushed and dumbfounded.

The enormity of utter hurt and betrayal overwhelms you. Heaviness and tension overtake your mind, body and soul.

Time stands still as you ache and wither in agony – feeling like you're falling, spinning, sinking, gravitating and collapsing with nothing to reach out and hold onto.

The rug has been firmly ripped from beneath you. Your world turned upside down. It's like you're trapped in a prism, looking through a distorted kaleidoscope, another dimension. All that you thought you knew and were is gone. You feel like you're dying inside even experiencing physical pain. Your stomach is churning, you shake as you try to balance yourself and your whole existence fills you with dread.

It's onset is so brutal and abrupt, it hits you like a ton of bricks. Most experience a sudden mortifying panic attack – intense fear and discomfort increasing and peaking. Such sensations of palpitations, a pounding heart, sweating, shortness of breath, numbness, trembling and an overwhelming experience that your own entity is in danger and under threat. Losing control and falling apart, igniting your fight or flight response the combined physical and mental thoughts of terror makes it more frightening for the victim to experience.

You will get no closure, have no discussion, no mutual talk, no respect, no conversation or value for the time you spent together. No final talk or amicable ending. Don't expect any narrative that answers your questions or even an acknowledgement of your pain. No resolution or a conclusion with no compassion or remorse from your abuser.
We can see through their mask, we know their lies and secrets and they are scared that we will expose them for the fraud that they really are. They have to keep up their

fake reputation and appearances to the outside world, as we are now too risky to keep around. We have seen and know too much. They will protect themselves at any cost. Another reason the Narcissist cuts you out so sharply, easily and abruptly is because they see everything as black or white. Once you were all good in the beginning an extension, a part of themselves until now you're seen and labelled as all bad. You are of no further value, unimportant a separate enemy who needs to be shut down and made out to be the assassin. An object to be murdered off and treated as if you never even existed. Throughout the fake relationship enduring putdowns, demeaning and unacceptable bad behaviour that you put up with, why do you expect decency and closure now?

Nothing has changed nothing ever will, they don't care how you are feeling, don't care if you're suffering and on the edge and even in some cases suicidal at this point. The only thing they are feeling is being more powerful, their endless appetite fed with continuous supply always insatiable wanting more.
They will never take ownership or have remorse for the brutal end of the relationship. It was always going to happen, you were just never told the rules or given a preview copy of the full finished script.

While they were devaluing you, behind the sidelines they were also in the process of ensnaring another source of supply- your replacement!

They may have more than one in the que waiting to be slotted into your part and they haven't quite decided yet who will be given the star role of serving the Narcissist.

The object who looks the most juicy and appetising, who will sing the Narcissists praises the loudest will be chosen. The one who offers the most and has the best resources, whether to make them look good, for status, sex, money, attention, affection or to triangulate them with you.

Or just an object who is newer, fresher and shiner to play with as you are now naturally boring to the Narcissist after becoming old supply.

They want to feel and experience the chase and rush with a new supply who is completely unaware of the monster within. They are now complacent with you and need to source and seduce a new mirror to reflect their perfect false selves, as you are now too far cracked and damaged.

He/she have many understudies and standbys in the background being assessed and trained to readily step into your character once your discarded and axed from the Narcissists show.

# Chapter 5

# The discard is a compliment in disguise-

The discard is a blessing in disguise and the fact you are no longer useful and wanted by the Narcissist is a compliment. It means you got stronger and you had the courage to find the strength to start standing up for yourself and question your abuser. They can sense when you are waking up and slowly starting to arouse from the hazy concoction of drugs.

You have woken up and called them out on their B/S. You have stopped feeding the beast. Narcissists hate it when you are onto them and start to figure them out, it means they don't have the upper hand anymore and this levelling out scares them.

Maybe you have been objecting, challenging, speaking up for yourself and have stopped sweeping the abuse under the carpet. You have lately been opening your eyes and questioning your reality. The Narcissist fears this the most as it means they are losing a grip of you, losing control and struggling to get you to comply and obey like usual. Therefore, you now threaten the Narcissist's false world and you need to be extracted and discarded before you get to them first. This way the abuser feels like they have the final say, the final win in what was always a game.

Once this has happened it will feel devastating or maybe even a relief with mixed emotions. In time you will be grateful for this release and will realise the only way for you to trump this and to 'really be the winner' is to drop the ball, walk away and never look back. If your'e not in it anymore then they can't hook you back in. After all they can't play by themselves, that would be no fun, so now they have to go and find another player to entertain them. Let them. For you are now free and able to start putting yourself and your needs first. Your'e able to start picking up the pieces and get your life back on track.
Your free to care and give self-love while growing, thriving and becoming richer and in sync with your true self.

*One of the major key actions after you are free from the Narcissist's clutches, is that you must now implement NO CONTACT or Low Contact as much as possible if children are involved.*

The only way to come out of the darkness and into the light is to own and acknowledge that you were targeted, groomed and moulded into a perfect codependent to serve the Narcissist. You must come to realise for your own sanity and self-worth to help you and propel you out of the quicksand that your life, your purpose and your identity is never ever dependent on what someone else is or isn't doing. We are responsible for our own happiness and choices in life, we must accept ownership and give ourselves closure from the fact that we were entwined in a toxic dysfunctional relationship and we must accept this horrific reality to gain closure and acceptance to move forward and evolve into the unique, beautiful individuals that we were meant to be all along. Start by turning this traumatic experience into a positive realisation that you are not what you went through and experienced, you are much more than that. You went through it to realise your own lack of self-worth, self-love and poor boundary functions which partly attracted and enabled this horrendous experience to occur. You now have the knowledge and resources to become fulfilled and dedicated to yourself in order to create the life you were always meant to achieve and align with.

Once you learn to grow and empower yourself, climbing out of hopelessness and into the light, you will start to believe and value yourself and in essence you will start to effortlessly attract people of the same calibre and dignity who will add value and substance to life. You will no longer obsess or accept anyone who treats you badly or disrespects you in any way in your life. You will only welcome genuine, healthy, normal, kind and supportive individuals who add meaning to your already authentic true self. You will naturally attract similar characters and qualities that you yourself posses, shuning and rejecting anything below your now high standards. Now is the time to embrace this traumatic event and confront the daily struggles and turn a hopeless experience and difficult time into an amazing life, changing the negative situation into a positive transformation like a caterpillar emerging into a splendid butterfly. A magical rainbow appearing after a heavy thunderstorm. Taking that first step no matter how small is your beginning to freedom, as you start to understand that failure leads you closer to success and miracles. It opens more doors and gives you unlimited opportunities to grow and to become whole. The obstacles of your past can become the gateways that lead you to more new fulfilling paths and direct you to your destiny.

# Chapter 6

## Letting go of toxic love-

You are now aware that in the beginning they went from charming and disarming to ultimately princess/prince harming.

All along they were shapeshifters morphing into your ideal man/woman. Possibly starting off very subtly, passive aggressively and cohesive behaviour turning more and more into controlling overt abuse as time went on.

Sometimes it's hard to realise you're in an unhealthy toxic relationship and how abuse isn't always physical. Emotional and psychological abuse can often be just as extreme and damaging, sometimes even more so. We need to educate people that having a lack or absence of physical violence does not mean the abuse is any less dangerous to the victim, in fact the long-term effects can be even more far reaching. Narcissists are masters of deception and manipulation getting the victim to believe it's all their fault. To the outsider it may come across trivial if you ever try to explain what's going on, but it is anything but.

When one partner constantly puts down, patronises another, blames the other for his or her faults, demeans

and belittles all your achievements, wears you down emotionally to keep you off balance, ignores you and shuts down your wants and needs, you end up being enveloped by a cloud of toxicity. They can also gain pleasure by ridiculing and mocking you, scolding you for having emotions and feelings, keeping tabs on the other's activities and trying to get their own way by playing the victim card you must begin to realise that this is not a healthy mutual loving relationship.

Their plan is to keep you reliant and dependent on them and to retain you trapped and locked in this toxic cycle.
As we are only seen and used as replaceable objects we are interchangeable and disposable to the Narcissist at any given time they see fit. A ticking time bomb waiting to inevitably be discarded and emotionally killed off. We can't hang on in hope anymore expecting things to change when nothing else changes and stays the same going around and around in a vicious circle repeating the same old dance.
This madness is keeping you stuck in a futile dead end of a so called relationship. It is unproductive, degrading and will always leave you feeling empty with your needs · forever being unmet.

We are survivors, warriors having a voice and are autonomous beautiful beings. We must take back our own power and control that which we freely handed over to our abuser and realise that we do deserve much more than this and to give ourselves the chance and self-respect to either decide it's a million times better to be on our own or the opportunity to go on and find a healthy relationship with someone who can truly love us and accept us for who we are.

# Chapter 7

# Who or What is the Narcissist?

Unfortunately, Narcissists are everywhere in our society, they blend in well to this environment, as remember they are always outwardly wearing a mask, which is made to hide the monster within.

This false cover-up also goes in the abusers favour as people on the outside can only vouch for the "nice guy/girl act/mask". So, when the victim starts to speak up to people around them they will not be believed and will be seen to be the crazy one. Outsiders have been fooled, tricked and deceived into this false belief. There is a stark contrast between the Narcissist's public and private selves.

A lot of Narcissists are in high powered jobs, positions of authority, exerting dominance and control. They can be overbearing when demonstrating importance of their successes. They are intelligent and can influence the behaviour, thoughts or the course of events of others, always with the underlying agenda of them gaining something from someone.

Although Narcissists are not always in high status positions they literally can be anyone from Joe next door, Sheila who works at the post office to Edward the waiter.

They can also be individuals in honest, charitable or caring roles where you automatically handover your belief and faith in them as they are in a position of confidence, credibility and trust.

Like victims, abusers can come from all professions, ethnic backgrounds, cultures, class and religions.

They are skilled and masters of deception and can hide their abuse even more so in this way. The ultimate game to portray themselves as a model citizen.

*The abusers live among us while hiding in plain sight.*

Having past experience of abandonment and unhealed scars of childhood trauma they lay dormant and suppressed until they bubble up and provoke the monster to erupt and then they desperately try to control their present reality. He/she wants a human doll/puppet who will submissively act out their fantasy of what and how a woman/man should be in their false idealistic world.

Behind their ultra confident exterior, there is a hidden dark secret. They are deeply insecure, flawed and lacking. Every move and action that the Narcissist makes is in his/her own best interest. All the odd, hurtful, cruel even at times dangerous actions, they rationalise it, always blaming the victim for the abuse. Never taking responsibility or accountability for their own choices. The Narcissist wants, needs to create their own perfect world on the outside at least; as they are forever avoiding their real inner damaged selves.

A lot of the dysfunctional behaviour the Narcissist carries out is unconscious and they are continuingly doing it out of habit without stopping to think about it. It's like driving a car, once you have passed your test and got your license to drive you continue to go on auto-pilot. I think the more self-aware ones who are conscious, have moments of awareness and know what they are doing is wrong but still feel compelled to carry on and cause further destruction.

A great number also get a sadistic kick out of knowing what they are doing and like to play dumb fuelling their manipulative streak that they can gain the upper hand and pull the wool over you, playing you like a fiddle.

# Chapter 8

# History and disorder of Narcissism-

The term 'Narcissism' comes from the Greek myth about Narcissus who was very proud and disdained those who loved him; so the Gods punished him by making him fall in love with his own image reflected back to him in a pool of water. Unable to leave the beauty of his reflection he lost his will to live and stared at his reflection until he died never knowing the meaning of true love or how to love others. It echoes the pursuit for self-gratification, extreme vanity, egocentricity, fixation on admiration and excessive selfishness for one's own attributes.

**Narcissistic Personality Disorder** is a condition that came into use in 1968 and the personality was first described in 1925 by Robert Waelder. In 1980 **NPD** was officially recognised in the third edition of the diagnostic and statistical manual of mental disorders which is used by many mental health care professionals to diagnose this disorder today. Individuals with (**NPD**) are characterised by their self-absorption, manner in which they exploit and take advantage of people around them, a superiority complex, excessive need for admiration and personal disdain for and lack or complete absence of empathy for other people. It usually develops in adolescence or during early adulthood. The actions and behaviours are very severe and can have a great negative destructive impact on those closest to the person with the disorder. The mind of someone with **NPD** is so twisted and impaired it's almost impossible for them to develop and sustain a true meaningful human close relationship.

*Signs and characteristics of a Narcissist- I have listed the most common ones which are trademark to the Narcissist as well as adding my own from personal experience-*

- They feel they are above others
- Come across as grandiose and superior
- Self absorbed and self centred
- Highly conceited
- Very Shallow
- No depth or substance
- Superficial
- Arrogant
- Fussy
- Moody
- Attention seeking
- Emotionally draining
- Childlike in their tantrums
- Monopolises conversations
- Redirects everything back to them
- Constantly trying to top trump you
- Highly competitive
- Blunt
- Poor listeners
- Think they're above the law or rules
- Very manipulative
- Dealing with them feels like hard work
- Demanding and entitled to the best treatment
- Always fishing for compliments
- Very negative
- Have no remorse or a conscience
- Have no empathy
- Only cares about him/herself
- Has genuine contempt for others
- Is a user
- Never wrong- always someone else's fault
- Perpetually bored
- Beyond selfish
- Impulsive
- Envious of others

So, Narcissism occurs on a spectrum with healthy self-esteem at one end and the pathological **Narcissistic Personality Disorder** at the other. As I have mentioned earlier I have been in romantic intimate relationships with two Narcissists who played out the same toxic unhealthy patterns but were also different in their methods and characteristics, which was shown more so in the beginning when I was love bombed and idolised.

In the first stage of dating their approaches and styles were somewhat different. However, the devaluation and discard cycle were eerily too similar and they could of been carried out by the same person, all the abuse was the same just a different mask and a different location.

The first abuser was a **Covert Vulnerable Narcissist.** From the first date mirroring me exactly and excessively, flattering me, homing in on admiring and idolising me for a few weeks/months in continual over the top love bombing and putting me high up on a pedestal.

Flowers, chocolates, gifts, compliments, talk of marriage/children, phone calls, handwritten letters, tattoo with my name, proposing, wanting to see me 24/7, all in an over the top obsessive way. Saying he couldn't live without me, I was his soulmate, some days he would phone in sick to work as he couldn't bare to be apart from me. Wanting to know my every move, who I was with and what I was doing.

He made a massive effort to the outside world to be this kind, generous and caring being. He was the better actor out of the two Narcissists very good at pretending, shape shifting into whatever anyone wanted him to be. These Narcissists are the hardest to spot as they are so good at pretending to get what they want, they are masters of a wolf in sheep's clothing. Both behind closed doors, when the initial idolisation wears off and they go into devaluation mode they start to show their true colours. This is when you will see they are very scarily alike and perform the same abuse techniques of gaslighting, blaming, put downs, criticising, belittling, hot/cold, push/pull dances, silent treatments etc all come into play and it's like the Narcissist is following the same script.

The second abuser was an **Overt Grandiose Narcissist.**
He was much easier to spot, recognise and notice the red flags earlier on which luckily it meant that I didn't waste or invest (anywhere) as near the same time as with the first one and dodged a bullet.
Being overt they can barely hide or suppress their self-obsessed and lack of empathic characteristics.
I remember my first date, he was still the charismatic charming guy but the bragger, the know-it-all one who monopolised the whole conversation and top trumped me on every interaction and communication.
I listened/he spoke, he bragged, gloated and kept re-directing the conversation back to him at every given opportunity. He was very confident, opinionated and enjoyed gaining my attention to listen attentively to his crowning accomplishments and self-pity stories. He was very excitable, like a little puppy and made plenty of eye contact and gestures of an intense connection between

us. He had high status in a professional job and he was also very good looking. He knew this only too well and enjoyed boasting about being smarter, better looking, more powerful, talented and superior than everyone else. He was an exhibitionist and loved the attention and validation from others. Over a couple of months he was carelessly rude about people, treating them nice and pleasant to their faces but then putting them down and slagging them off behind their backs.

Then over a short period of time the confident happy-go-lucky facade began to fade and a dark, cold, aloofness being instead crossed my path. He was getting more and more inconsistent saying one thing and doing another, watching me get so frustrated and confused by the sudden hot and cold dances. His sense of entitlement was always present from work to family life. He was arrogant and boastful needing to be the best at everything and prove to being intellectually superior all the time and at any cost. He was smug when outsmarting others and bragged about being better and smarter than those he associated with. Constantly saying how unappreciated he felt and how nobody understood his specialness and his uniqueness. He was also extremely competitive whether competing against a grown man like himself or with a child- it didn't matter, his only goal was to win.

Every interaction felt like a competition or tournament. It was exhausting he would never be happy for others successes or achievements, only gloat if they failed and lost. He would talk down to you in a condescending manner, treating his opinions as fact and everyone else's as wrong and not knowing what they're talking about. For he thought he was god-like and of course in turn knew everything about anything. He would rage at other drivers, berate waiters/waitresses expecting special treatment in restaurants and generally putting down and belittling others. He was addicted to social media, relying on receiving constant attention from strangers, acquaintances and friends. It didn't matter who just as long as he was being admired and externally validated. He travelled abroad at every opportunity due to boredom and being constantly unsatisfied.

Always having over the top expectations and this in turn naturally ending up being disappointed. Not only obsessed with his intelligence but also preoccupied with power and success, very fickle constantly chopping and changing decisions/thoughts about jobs, careers, life, friends or which country to live in. He imagined he was perfect and wanted only to mix and associate with other perfect beings. He had a massive ego and didn't care about being arrogant or outspoken. He openly would be rude and haughty to outsiders but kept his cruelty and extreme selfishness and contempt for those nearest and dearest behind closed doors, where he felt comfortable to rip his mask off and let the abuse and games begin.

He was also a **Cerebral Narcissist** (*obsessed with his brain*) who relied on his intelligence to attract and secure women. He had a belief he was knowledgeable on just about any topic. A storyteller showing off his unique brilliance. They tend to be asexual and after securing Narcissistic supply will pull away physically and withdraw affection imaging they are far too superior and god-like to have an intimate closeness with another human being. As in their minds common beings do the deed, they only pretend to get close to you in the beginning as they understand that most humans act this way so they do it as a means to an end to hook you in then pull away once they know your addicted.

The first abuser on the other hand was a **Somatic Narcissist** (*obsessed with his body*), the complete opposite.
He wasn't intelligent or in a high status powered job, he was consumed and preoccupied with physical beauty and prowess. He loved the gym and showing off his muscles and physique and boasting about his sexual conquests.
So even though one was obsessed with his physical appearance and the other obsessed with his intelligence they were both mechanical in their gestures, actions romantically and otherwise robotic and unemotional.

*Traits and actions BOTH Narcissists had in common and carried out-*

- Found it entertaining to set people up and watch them fail and fall
- Enjoyed creating and provoking drama and chaos, pulling the strings and thriving off of a victims weakness
- Creating and causing drama, then turning around- saying they 'hate drama'!
- Played the hot/cold dance
- Both played the victim card- stories of their ex's cheating, crazy psychos who took advantage of the Narcissists, who didn't understand them, who took from them and none of it was their fault in the demise of the relationships
- Highly manipulative learning how to push other people's buttons and using different tactics to gain the upper hand and take control
- Neither had integrity or any empathy
- Were moody, perpetually bored, underlyingly miserable and had negative attitudes behind closed doors
- If you were ill they were even more cold, indifferent and disdained, treating you as a weak inconvenient nuisance. Even getting a glass of water was too much trouble as the attention was now on the sick person, which they absolutely hate as any distraction or situation is taking away the

focus, light and attention from them god-like selves

- Being a 'victim' neither would ever take responsibility or accountability for their own life and actions. All their past mistakes and misfortunes were everyone else's fault, never theirs
- Both carried out the Devaluation and Discard cycle in a predictable manner. Using lying, blame shifting, silent treatments, gaslighting and withholding affection to get what they wanted, (hence why I didn't spend long in my second Narcissistic relationship as I had already experienced and seen the signs of the Devalue and Discard stages with the first one; I could see it all clearly the second time around)
- Both enjoyed playing friends against one another knowing they were the cause of arguments and destruction
- Thoroughly enjoyed exploiting others with no remorse or a conscience
- Both would not apologise (only the first one would fake apologise to get me re-hooked in the cycle)
- Both were very impatient and irritable especially whilst shopping, queuing or having to wait for anything
- Only cared about themselves and getting their own needs met
- Neither could take feedback about their bad behaviour as it was a threat to their false-self

- Both blamed others for their problems
- Inability to emotionally support you
- Talked a lot about quitting jobs to work with people who will appreciate them, forever saying they had options whether in careers or with woman to make me feel insecure to keep me on my toes and off balance to remind me of how easy it is to be replaced at anytime
- Both were demanding and child like, wanting continuous attention and praise
- Compulsive liars
- Both would trianglate to inflict fear, create jealousy and to make it obvious I was disposable
- Would create tension so it felt like you were walking on eggshells
- Emotionally absent

# Chapter 9

# The False-self VS The True-self

## *False-self*

The Narcissist has constructed a pretence false-self, which they portray to the outside world. Over time they have tried to perfect this fake image to fool the world and themselves that they are this great, wonderful person who is utterly superior and special, a unique being who deserves the best treatment to be loved and admired excessively. They continually look for external validation to prop up their home-made mask and to support their own fantasies and delusions about themselves. They are constantly on stage, observing their audience, always acting and playing a role. They expect complete compliance from their audience and characters as they see themselves as the most important star in their own 'show'.

Everyone is a prop to be used and abused, and everyone has a shelf life, an expiry date, which comes sooner rather than later if you ever question or challenge the Narcissists falsely constructed, fragile distorted mask. They will do anything to protect this fabricated, deceptive and phoney illusion, even lying to themselves just to keep the show going.

Due to this fake scaffolded construction and made up image, they are extremely untrustworthy, disloyal, two-faced, hypocritical, backstabbing, hollow and shallow. They are scam artists cheating and tricking others by persuading them to believe their false persona. It's a confidence trick, to defraud a person and gain their trust. Masters at exploiting others characteristics such as compassion, naivetey, vulnerability and empathy. Now those can be good traits to have but can also be dangerous when in the wrong hands.

In the Idealisation stage when they are grooming you, they can be over the top with tunnel-vision, homing in on you as their prey. They are only interested in you (for their own gratification) and therefore in order to suck you in they pull out all the stops to make you feel very special and wanted. However, once you are no longer a challenge and they have secured your love and trust, they start to pull away as they've gotten what they wanted or become bored with you and will now either abandon you without a backward glance or toy with you for a bit longer until they are ready to emotionally push you off a cliff.

A Narcissist can be very funny, engaging and sociable as long as you are fulfilling their script and what they desire at that moment in time. They are emotional vampires who want to suck all your attention and energy and exhaust you untill you are empty, thus now becoming inconvenient, useless and needing to be disposed of. Narcissists are like ticks, they are parasites living and existing by feeding on (blood) aka your energy and once latched on they drain you dry gorging on your resources until their bodies are satisfied and full. They do this to survive and move from one host to another. They die eventually if unable to find a host. Another similar association with a parasite is that they can spread disease once remaining attached to their host. These analogies are exactly the same concept of how a Narcissist behaves. They are the tick and you, the victim are their host. They are only using you as a means to an end.

When a Narcissist is criticised they feel like they are under attack and their carefully constructed world is being threatened. They will either rage in defensiveness or shun you with utter contempt.

So, now we know how and why Narcissists construct this False-Self, the next question we can ask ourselves is who is the 'real' person behind the mask?

# *True-self*

The answer is parallel to what they are falsely projecting onto the world. Deep down they are insecure, scared empty beings. They have this constant need to have their imaginary greatness validated and verified by external resources. When reality catches up with them they may react by becoming depressed and even more detached. They have an underlying absence of self and shame residing in their inner core. Since a young age they disassociated and detached themselves from their true selves. Theories behind this suggest it was a self-defence mechanism to protect themselves in order to survive in their hostile environment. They may of had an inconsistent experience with their main caregivers for instance. Parents who refused to acknowledge achievements, always expecting more and more from their child, instills a sense that they are never quite good enough and end up always striving to please others.

In most cases with pathological disorders there is a question of nature versus nurture. In this instance, whether Narcissists were made or born that way. It is difficult to say for sure, most experts agree that these two things are combined and a catalyst to producing an individual with **NPD**. So, a combination of genes and environmental factors seem likely. Other factors can influence this dynamic such as social and cultural beliefs and expectations. One theory is that children can tend to adopt Narcissistic traits if they are overvalued and treated like a trophy – encouraging and pushing them to be competitive and always strive to be/do more than their best. This magnified their focus on never losing and being successful no matter what and puts a great deal of stress and pressure of unreachable and unachievable expectations and goals for the child to achieve.

In turn, the child is acting like a circus monkey on display forever trying to win their parents love and affection resulting in the creation of an insecure attachment with conditions and over the top expectations which no one can live up to.

Another theory opposing the first one is that a child has been exposed to neglectful parenting. The child is abandoned either physically or emotionally. The trauma of being physically or mentally rejected starts a catalyst for self-destruction especially if the child is young and hasn't developed their own sense of self yet. As minors we rely on receiving this connection from mirroring our parents and getting feedback that shapes and sustains our ego. Without it we are completely lost in the world struggling to fit in and feel like we don't belong anywhere. It makes the child feel like they are loners, shut off from the world and humanity, having no purpose or value in life. They internalise this abandonment as a reflection of themselves and in turn start thinking that they must be to blame. They feel unlovable, worthless, a burden – it fills them with doubt and shame, struggling to find balance and self worth. Lost souls searching for some kind of meaning and attachment. Wanting desperately to belong and be accepted for who they are. In their minds if their own parents ignore, ridicule and shun them, then who do they have left, they can't trust anyone or anything. If the people who brought them into this world, are meant to love and protect them but instead treat them with indifference and disapproval then no one can be trusted, everyone is to be feared and be sceptical of. They are taught that being open and vulnerable is scary and dangerous. No good comes from it only pain, hurt and heartache. So, they can never allow themselves to become close to anyone, never form intimate meaningful deep relationships only fake superficial ones. Anything else is too risky for their fragile egos. They feel wounded, powerless and helpless, thus resulting in the false mask being constructed and executed.

# Chapter 10

# The abuse techniques and arsenal of weapons the Narcissist uses against you-

Being in an emotional, psychological or physical war zone can leave victims so broken and dysfunctional themselves that they can lose everything – from careers, children, homes, friends, family, money even down to their "*self*". Once the honeymoon/love bombing stage declines, the Narcissist now becomes comfortable that they can start the devaluation phase by using different tricks and games to keep you off balance and more dependent on them. For the Narcissist this is where the fun now begins, as they can toy with your emotions and punish you in unfathomable ways. By spinning your reality this in turn makes their warped one feel safer. They will do whatever it takes to keep control over you. Narcissists are like some pretty flowers they may seem compelling and beautiful on the outside but once close-up can be deadly. Just like a rose may outwardly look beautiful and inviting to pick, it is also armed with sharp prickles and thorns. That being mixed with another tempting beauty like 'the lily of the valley', which is very toxic if eaten. The flowers, leaves and stems contain cardiac glycosides, which act directly on the heart and cause vomiting, illusions, blurriness and can be fatal in some cases. The poison is slowly absorbed into the body and gradually released in the same way an abuser infects and drip-feeds you venomous negative mind viruses. Starting off as seeds that inevitably begin to grow and hijack your brain. They implant mind parasites to slowly spread and eat away and take over your mind, body and soul. As the victim, once infected you will believe things which are outright false or contradictory. You will begin to accept bad treatment and demeaning behaviour. You will minimise, rationalise and justify your abusers horrific treatment. You will gradually succumb to frequent threats, broken promises, future faking, nasty tricks and out right personal attacks. The Narcissist is so good at infecting you with unwanted programming and self-destructive behaviours. They are masters of deception and manipulation and carry a bag full of weapons to ultimately destroy you. It is brainwashing at its greatest and takes away your freedom and the essence of who "YOU" are.

They introduce unwelcome thoughts and ideas- as well as trying to change your attitudes, values and beliefs. Spreading poisonous words to cloud your judgement, to take away your independent thinking and own unlimited beliefs. Once latched on, it over rides our logical thinking ability and is replaced with confusing actions, which lead us to do things that we would not on a rational basis have done or put up with otherwise. They change your mental state and balance by infecting you with horrendous acts of abuse and create turbulence. This makes you easier to co-operate, mould and control, to then establish what you can and cannot do, what the Narcissist perceives as acceptable or unacceptable from you- they are training you into full and complete submission. The weapons they use are to keep you in your place, not to question or answer them back. They are injected to demonstrate and uphold dominance over you and show you who's the leader to follow, the boss who runs the show.

Below are a list of common weapons and abuse the Narcissist will use to keep you under their power and influence.

In my next chapter, I discuss in more detail about each of these cruel, degrading and repetitive lethal weapons they use against you as continuous ammunition.

1. Gaslighting
2. Blame-shifting
3. Projection
4. Stonewalling / Silent treatment
5. Rage
6. Verbal abuse
7. Physical abuse
8. Passive / Aggressive behaviour
9. Hot / Cold cycles

# Chapter 11

# Gaslighting-

Gaslighting is a common form of abuse in psychological and emotional abusive relationships. It is where information and reality is intentionally manipulated to make the victim doubt his/her own perception and question their own sanity. The abuser does this in many subtle or obvious ways, such as telling you that the things you've seen, heard or experienced are a figment of your imagination. By doing so the Narcissist gains complete control and submissiveness. By creating these deliberate scenarios and circumstances, you then automatically appear as if you are losing your mind, you're the 'crazy one', erratic and unstable, overly emotional and sensitive.

The abuser's actions are deliberate and insidious. They know exactly what they are doing by creating situations where you appear to be confused and unstable. This trickery clouds your usual clear judgement, as the longer it continues you go on doubting yourself and end up even more dependent on the abuser. In turn trusting more of what the perpetrator tells you is real and ignoring and dismissing your own true perceptions. They create this confusing mindset, sending you into a tail-spin and therefore setting you up to come across as a crazy person out of character and control who is losing their mind. Slowly, over time you begin to lose more and more of yourself as they chip away at your confidence and reality. The effects of this make you cling to the Narcissist even more so, relying on them to steer and be in control of you, as you are now so broken and incapable of making independent decisions on your own. The more 'apparent' mistakes and misfortunes you make, the more control and power you handover to the Narcissist. Their aim is for you to completely and utterly succumb to their higher authority so they can continue to push your buttons and pull your strings. You end up being nothing more than a 'human toy' to be abused, manipulated and played with in a cat and mouse game, which is played over and over again. He/she is the spider weaving a web of lies and traps and you as the victim are the poor innocent fly.

The term Gaslight came originally in 1938 from Patrick Hamilton's play 'Gaslight'. A couple of years later it was turned into film adaptations and has since been used in clinical and research literature. In the film it portrays a husband slowly distorting his wife's reality, sowing seeds of doubt to make her question her own memory, perception and sanity. The husband manipulates her so much she believes she's going insane. This is exactly one of the same tactics in which the Narcissist abuses his/her victim, by using persistent denial, misdirection, contradiction and lying. I was Gaslighted myself in numerous situations into believing things that never happened in order to distort and control my beliefs and my true reality. One vivid personal example of gaslighting by my abuser was one time in a lift. He was being his usual hot/cold distant self and I wanted to start the day afresh with no bad atmosphere so I said let's draw a line under today and start again and went to kiss him on the lips. I remember him staring down at me with cold dark vacant eyes and the look of contempt sprawled across his face as he pulled away from my attempt to kiss and make up. Only 10 minutes later we were in a cafe drinking coffee and I asked why he was acting so weird and aloof and why he turned me down trying to lock lips with him earlier and he turned around to me straight face and said *"I don't know what your talking about, I did kiss you"*, in that moment it hit me how cruel and horrific he sounded knowing full well he hadn't. The fact it had only taken place 10 minutes before was shocking how easy it was for him to blatantly lie to my face.

This is only one example of what my Narcissists were capable of, they loved staging and setting up scenarios to disorientate the truth of what happened. This is one of their favourite games and weapons to use against you. They deliberately lie seamlessly and contradict themselves to create doubt and control in the relationship. On top of this if you do speak back with the real truth, an argument will erupt causing more negative drama and gives them more leeway into attacking projecting, blaming and twisting everything around onto you; so, it's a win/win situation for the Narcissist.

When this starts to happen regularly it makes you question your own sanity and pushes you to rely on your abuser for the truth, which is of course non-existent as they have invented it all from the beginning. By them making up, withholding information, discounting the truth, verbal abuse and undermining and point blank ignoring you plus saying what had occurred in fact hadn't, it would make anyone doubt their senses and mind.

After all you are meant to be in a close relationship to this person, therefore surely your partner that you care about and love, you can ultimately trust?

Unfortunately this so-called bond strengthens the abusers hold as you want so much to believe them and in the end by them gradually weakening you and your thought process they are slowly brainwashing you, so you give up your entire identity, thoughts, feelings and actions. The abuser may hide things from you and then cover up and deny knowing anything about it. They may also try to isolate you from friends and family so that the abuser has full influence and control over you without the risk of you getting any help or validation from outside sources, which further leaves you dependent on the abuser. As the abuse usually starts off slow you may not at first glance begin to notice it. Very slowly and gradually it eats away at your ability to make sound judgements and be confident in what you see and hear.

The Narcissist spins their negative and harmful words or actions in their favour, to deflect their true intentions and actions and then blame the victim all the while pointing the finger at you saying you're 'paranoid', 'overly sensitive', 'over reacting', 'dramatic', 'crazy' and many other cruel words, which causes you to even more doubt yourself and your reality.

It becomes a downhill struggle as you frequently begin to second-guess yourself and your ability to remember the details of past events. You may also be so worn down and emotionally and mentally drained that you find yourself apologising for the things deemed to be wrong in your relationship. You feel anxious, misunderstood and depressed. Finding it hard to make even simple decisions as you have been told so many times by your abuser that events didn't happen, that you start to distrust yourself.

Behind closed doors the perpetrator wears you down so much by continuingly discrediting and invalidating you and your experiences that they can now begin to shame, humiliate and undermine you in public to portray you as the disturbed and crazy one. They may stage a scene, knowing full well it will get you to overreact and cause a confrontation. They immediately may jump at you by denying any understanding of what you're talking about and trivialise and minimalise your experience. Acting in a very calm and controlled way to make you even more look like the loony one out of place.

By twisting and reframing what was said or done it supports their illusion of you even more so being the one losing your mind. They may also change the subject to divert and create more confusion and say things like "you're imagining things, that never happened", "I never said or did that", "you're wrong, you don't remember it right", " you need to see someone about this", "you're pushing me away", "your behaviour is very worrying" as they sometimes cloak their fake compassion to make out they're worried about you and on your side.

It is a dangerous form of abuse guaranteed to erode the victims mental balance, self, confidence and self-esteem. It undermines the mental stability of the victim who can eventually become withdrawn, drained, depressed and even suicidal.

# Chapter 12

# Blame shifting-

Blame shifting is a common weapon used by emotional manipulators and I call it the 'blame game'. The sole purpose for this is to avoid and spin the blame from the Narcissist onto the victim. Twisting around the blame of their misbehaviour to project it onto you and instead focus on your 'reactions' to their bad behaviour. This means the Narcissist avoids taking responsibility or accountability for their appalling abuse. They are setting it up to spin reality and wash their hands of any wrongdoing. This popular attack by the Narcissist is frustrating and confusing for the victim. Every conversation, act and situation can get twisted around and put upon you, now making it your fault for what or why something happened. Remember he/she cannot bear to be criticised or own upto their mistakes as this then means they are less than perfect. Everything to them is about winning and any interaction with them is a competition or tournament. They do not understand or comprehend the word 'compromise' or owning their own part in a negative situation.

Where two healthy individuals will sit down calmly and discuss each other's part in a dispute or argument and both put their hands up and accept equal responsibility in it, the Narcissist will do no such thing. Immediately their back goes up like a scared cat trapped and cornered by a fox and they are ready on the attack – pointing the finger at you for everything that's gone wrong.

Everything is your fault, if only you had done or said this or acted in a different or certain way you wouldn't be in this situation. If only you had listened to the Narcissist in the first place and followed what they had said then you wouldn't be in this mess. You may automatically try to defend yourself but it's futile as he/she will have an arsenal of reasons why this has come about. Old and new conversations will appear from nowhere, every mistake you ever made you will be reminded of and they will be brought up. Every problem that ever arose in your relationship you will be accused of creating. This forces the blame onto you and deflects away from the Narcissist. They will wear you down so much you will forget the original reason of what you were trying to discuss in the first place.

The Narcissist knows you're compassionate and empathetic and will exploit your sympathy and concern in any way they see fit. The truth is they don't care if you are upset or that your feelings got hurt and the more you try to explain or reason with them, the more angry and irritated they will get. You will be classed as the selfish one, the ungrateful one, the needy one who is demanding and acting like a spoiled brat, when all you started off wanting was a simple two-way reciprocal and respectful conversation from your partner. It turns into World War I and you're left trying to safely detonate the hidden mines and fight your way through confusion and unmerited accusations and lies. It literally feels as if you are trying to navigate and survive being in a minefield. The Narcissist is so good at laying booby traps and distorting reality.

Often blame shifting occurs when they have experienced a Narcissistic injury or a healthy boundary was set by the victim and therefore the abuser now feels so out of control, sensing a loss of power. To override this crippling anxiety they try and 'turn the tables' to once again gain the upper hand. They are so good at portraying themselves as the 'victim' and you being the problem. They can't fathom themselves having any flaws and by them believing they are right at all times, they can just about manage to cling onto their false image. Even when they clearly and obviously did something wrong it will never be acknowledged as their responsibility or fault. They must at all costs deflect the blame onto the victim who they use as a scapegoat for their internal and external failures. You will be made to feel like it is all your fault and you are the one who must end up apologising to the abuser. So, not only are you held liable for the whole blaming scenario but you will also be blamed and shamed for expressing yourself and having legitimate feelings and trying to defend yourself and have a voice. How dare you act and respond in a normal, mature adult manner. It is unacceptable to question the God almighty Narcissist and have an opposing opinion.

You are there as an emotional doormat to take away their buried shame and deep-seated wounds. You're there to absorb and digest their errors with no resolution. Narcissists are expects at shifting and feel that they are not culpable for their words or actions when they clearly are. In their sick minds, no matter what has really happened, they rationalise and justify it. As victims are well known to be empaths, they in turn are likely to accept, become subservient and turn a blind eye in order to keep the peace and continually cover up and undertake the culpability that isn't theirs to own.

# Chapter 13

## *Projection-*

Projection is similar to blame shifting. It's usually an unconscious transfer of the Narcissist's unwanted desires or emotions onto the victim. They do this to protect their false self and it is another defence mechanism that they use to deflect and blame the victim for their bad thoughts and unbearable feelings. By placing their unacceptable feelings onto another they are refusing to accept them as their own and are projecting feelings of their inferiority and deep-seated fears.

An example of projection from my personal experience with a Narcissist was as soon as I was starting to stand up for myself, question and challenge my abuser he turned around and projected all his crap onto me. He vomited out an avalanche of hurtful comments of the things he was doing and feeling, saying I was 'moody', 'ungrateful', 'manipulative' and 'played mind games'- which of course was exactly the identical things he was responsible of doing but he refused to accept ownership of these characteristics and abuse tactics and instead mirrored them on to me. By him spewing his own attributes onto another, he was releasing all accountability and making it instead belong and stick to myself. Their own flawed character traits are disowned and shone brightly onto you. Whatever it is that the Narcissist doesn't like about themselves, they try to banish and assign onto you. Poisonous words roll off their forked tongue like a venomous snake. It could be anything like saying 'you are fat', 'ugly', 'boring', 'selfish', 'useless', 'stupid'- whatever it is the abuser is feeling at the time. Basically all their weaknesses, disowned wounds, verbal diarrhoea and vile abuse will be reflected onto another.

Another example is if your partner is cheating. They may turn around and accuse you of infidelity but it is in fact themselves that is carrying out this despicable behaviour. By them blaming you and assigning their dysfunctional and broken parts onto you it has now been deflected from them and the subject is now focused on your invented bad behaviour. If successful and the victim doesn't protest to accepting these false truths, then the Narcissist is released of these unwanted impulses, unpleasant feelings and dirty actions reducing their anxiety and discomfort. This makes them get away with anything, not being culpable for any unacceptable behaviour. They will accuse you of doing and being all sorts of 'crazy' that you instinctively and logically know you didn't do or say. If you don't willingly absorb these disowned accusations the Narcissist will fight tooth and nail to remain unaccountable and to pin all blame at your feet.

# Chapter 14

# Silent Treatment / Stonewalling-

In the past I have been involved with two different Narcissists. The first one's favourite weapon was **rage** while the second abuser's chosen one was giving me the **silent treatment.** They are both tactics to get you to obey and punish you to complete compliance. The silent treatment is a calculated, cold, robotic move to express disapproval and contempt for any perceived slights. By the abuser consistently and deliberately ignoring you, freezing you out and refusing to speak or even acknowledge your presence, they are asserting their dominance and authority. Shunning you and icing you out is in essence rejecting and abandoning the victim.

Personally, I found this one of the worst kinds of punishment as there is no room to negotiate, repair or even reason when on the receiving end. The total silence is torture and can be mind-boggling. Healthy relationships thrive on mutual open communication and trust, being able to talk and discuss anything and everything to find a resolution. When faced with ostracism it is pathological punishment at its greatest. It is meant to hurt you, it is meant to make you squirm, feel insignificant and designed so that you feel worthless and unlovable. It places the abuser in a position of control and avoids any attempt to resolve any conflict, take responsibility or compromise.

By them asserting their cold icy silence, the message actually screams volumes. It can leave the victim feeling frustrated, restless, anxious, lonely, isolated and depressed.

The Narcissist is denying your entire existence by fading you out and making you insignificant and invisible. Being ignored can leave you second-guessing yourself and doubting whether you really did something wrong in the relationship to cause this persistent treatment. It puts a very stressful strain on the victim and can heighten your *fight* or *flight* response as you are so uncertain of when it is going to end, when are they going to put you out of your misery and start communicating and acting in a normal manner to you again. Patterns of the silent treatment may get longer as time goes on into the relationship as the abuser ups the anti-and tightens their psychological grip on you. Spells of excluding and banishing you can be very harmful and disastrous to your health and well-being.

**Stonewalling** is refusing to communicate or cooperate. They may still express some communication even if minimal. They may either change the subject or deflect from the subject at hand or give sparse or vague responses. It puts a stop to a mutual, open listening dialogue and instead causes distance, added strain and conflict. They can also physically leave the room so there is no chance to discuss or to get to a joint resolution. It is usually a delaying tactic meant to buy time.

However, in the **silent treatment** there is no verbal communication whatsoever, you are completely erased out. Blacklisted, tuned out by the abuser refusing to make eye contact, unresponsive, turning away and even point blank ignoring you when in the same room. You are now nothing more than a *'ghost'* in the room. The abuser withdraws completely and utterly, while still acknowledging and talking to other people either in or out of your presence. It's a lesson to teach you to behave in future and keep you in check. Even if you haven't actually done anything wrong, in the Narcissist's damaged twisted mind they can perceive the slightest wrongdoing as a threat to their superiority. By disconnecting, switching off all contact is truly torturous when this is the person you deeply care about who is treating you in a horrific, disrespectful way knowing full well it is harming you. Their intent is to cause a shift in power and take the lead, causing insecurity and uncertainty. Wanting to be at the top of the hierarchy and to avoid losing control. They stay stone like, still as a statue as you may try to talk, beg, cry or scream at them.

They completely shut down, like when a computer is switched off. Any sign of you wanting to discuss an issue or becoming obviously upset has no effect on the Narcissist. They refuse to answer your questions, pretend they can't hear you, remain motionless, offering absolutely nothing. Being evasive of any efforts that you are trying to interact or trying to resolve the situation. They withhold verbal communication and also withdraw any affection so you are literally left out in the cold.

It can start off with mild bouts of silence growing into long torturous durations. The powerful message of exile and an icey distance cuts out any chance of correspondence or communication. Just because there is no screaming or hitting there is still plenty of violence and it is there to further frustrate and insult you.

Silence can be healthy when used in the right sense, to put the brakes on say a heated argument or to pause an intense conflict before it escalates. In healthy relationships you will both feel safe and be able to express wanting some temporary time out. You will both know it's short lived and when both calm and ready you can have a safe and secure dialogue to find solutions and resolutions to any disagreements.

*It becomes abusive when used to degrade, manipulate, punish and control you.*

# Chapter 15

# Rage-

When your abuser is in a full rage venting their anger, it is nearly impossible to stop them in their tracks. The red mist comes up and their beast within overrides them. They feel justified in their reaction of making you as distressed as possible and enjoy gaining a reaction from you, which in turn feeds their ugly monster. The abuser may appear to be out of control externally but internally they can actually feel quite calm and in control. For victims the constant state of worrying and wondering when the next rage is coming wreaks havoc on your health and mental stability. The effects of self-doubt and fear consume your body with stress hormones and has a negative impact on your mental and physical well-being.

My first Narcissist, who used rages frequently, was able to turn their behaviour on and off like a switch. Behind closed doors he would spew vile comments, spit, scream and at times start raging and throwing things around like a maniac. Then once having emptied his disgusting verbal attack he would go back to acting like nothing had happened after feeling a sense of detoxification once he had expelled his built up anger onto me.

This Jekyll & Hyde dynamic was my life for 16 years. I got so used to and immune from the constant rages that I was almost separate and desensitised from them after being exposed to them for so long.

By the Narcissist acting out, it is another form of control to gain the upper hand, scare you into submission, start or continue an argument and escalate it. They want you to lose your control so they can attack back and gain a position of power. If you do nothing and stay silent they will scream and demand you to answer them in order to create a chain of dramatic events so that they can continue to argue, vent and cause as much displeasure as possible.

Abusers are very good at choosing to time these outbursts and do so usually when you're alone with no one to witness their cruelty. This indeed is backed up by the fact they tend not to 'show' this side in public or when others are around and if someone outside shows up they can immediately become perfectly calm and quickly switch back to their logical, and rational fake mask. In the beginning idealization stage they would of tried really hard to curb these feelings from bubbling up and over spilling, as they know if they were to reveal their true colours too soon before you are hooked you wouldn't even contemplate a relationship with someone as aggressive and dysfunctional as themselves.

At times the rages stem from unconsciously being reminded of something that had enraged them in their past and they were powerless at the time to confront or stop it. Over time they buried and stored these negative, angry, resentful feelings inside and as a consequence now as adults feel compelled and safe to finally let loose and relay these inner demons onto someone weaker than them. It is a kind of 'temporary insanity', which bubbles up after lying dormant for so long and resurfaces and effectively is regurgitated onto the victim. Their self-righteous rage is a desperate defence mechanism used to protect them from further painful and vulnerable feelings, which may have come close to the surface after being triggered by something in the present environment. Sometimes by counteracting and responding in a similar manner to the Narcissist it may make them more enraged and prone to lash out physically. Once the fire burns out and it is safe to do so, trying to talk to the abuser about what has happened can also be futile.

In toxic relationships, they are not willing to discuss their outbursts in any meaningful way and out right will take no accountability or responsibility for their actions and will blame you for causing them to lose their grip and rage in the first place. If they do apologise it won't be sincere and genuine, it will be just lip service to keep you in the cycle of torment and abuse. It is inevitable, if they are prone to raging that it usually gets worse over time. Tensions and frustrations continue and episodes of rage are continually activated. Victims live on a constant edge of 'walking on eggshells' trying to prevent and avoid any outbursts. Trying to appeal to the Narcissist's good side and continually making an effort not to 'set them off' is draining and exhausting as the goalposts are forever moving. Rages can last from a few minutes to hours and can be very intense and frightening for the victim on the receiving end. The rage is part of the abuse cycle, whereby he/she may then try to make up with victim, to confuse and further hook them in with spells of contempt and silent treatments scattered throughout to really keep the victim on their toes and make them feel like they are constantly walking on 'hot stones'. The Narcissist's rages are like broken records on repeat, trying to gauge and get you to react.

From my own experiences it can start off over something so minor and trivial and then the abuser escalates it into a full-blown rage. They are so good at turning the slightest thing into a big deal just to cause havoc and drama, even something as minute for example as saying that a cup is facing the wrong way, or a pen is missing its lid. It doesn't matter what it is, he/she will always find something to pick on and start a fight over. It's a no-win situation for you and your only plan of action should be to leave the situation and not engage with them. Simply remove yourself and walk away. Do not tolerate this kind of bad behaviour and treatment, you deserve to be free and happy and feel safe and secure in a relationship. Not scared to rock the boat for having an opinion or even because you're breathing. You will be made to feel like everything you do is not good enough and you will be constantly in a state of tiptoeing around the Narcissist.

Emotionally blackmailed and living in fear from the pathological abuse, which no one should ever tolerate.

# Chapter 16

# Verbal Abuse-

Verbal attacks are very common when in unhealthy relationships. The abuser will launch into a barrage of put downs, aggressive name-calling, swearing, screaming and other derogatory remarks. It is used to wear you down and tear apart your self-worth and confidence. By verbally battering you and chipping away at your personality and characteristics, you are left beaten down and deflated.

Trying to have a normal, sincere conversation of healthy dialogue is impossible with a Narcissist. Each time you try to engage in a verbal exchange of words you may feel like you are about to disturb the viper's nest. They will start off slowly but in time use these tactics on a more regular basis, saying things such as "you're lazy", "you're putting on weight", "you can't cook", "you're driving wrong", "you are a psycho", "you are ungrateful", "you are useless" etc. Using words as weapons is meant to hurt and injure you and can be demonstrated in two ways. One is in an obvious and overt way such as open put downs, being sworn at, blamed, accusations and humiliation. Or subtle, covert ways such as hidden aggression, belittlement, sarcasm, insults disguised as jokes and nasty comments veiled as helpful tips and concern. By eroding your worth it shapes the way you start to view yourself.

Once you could do no wrong and now you're worthless, it must be all your fault to experience this sudden demoralising change from your partner. The abuser has a powerful need for dominance and unwillingness to accept their partner as an equal. It is manipulative and controlling coercive behaviour, which creates emotional pain and mental anguish in their victim. Cohesive control is the pattern of behaviour that seeks to take away and destroy the victims freedom and strip away their identity and sense of self. They get off on lecturing you like a small child, twisting and turning every conversation into a battle of words. They may also enjoy micromanaging you to monitor your behaviour and daily activities, dictate who you can and can not see, hint that your likes and tastes are all wrong, tell you what or how they prefer you to wear/dress and generally taking over your own choices, thoughts and desires. By them also discounting and invalidating your thoughts, feelings, perceptions and experiences this further undermines and causes you more psychological pain.

Slowly you begin to lose sight of the old you, who you were and just like a solar eclipse where the moon begins to partially block out the sun- your identity is slowly eroded piece by piece. Then gradually over time further segments of yourself get obscured and overshadowed by your abuser, until they fully conceal and block your shining bright light and you are left in total darkness.

Verbal abuse leaves you in fear of humiliation, failure, worthlessness or even fear of turning into abandonment or physical violence. Verbal bullying by your partner is carried out to make your abuser feel good, powerful and in control. You must try to stay grounded and not absorb their toxic words, which are distorted without merit. They are projecting their own vulnerabilities and insecurities onto you and their goal is for you to own them and accept them as your bad characteristics.

# Chapter 17

# Physical Abuse-

As well as victims enduring constant bouts of psychological, verbal, mental and emotional abuse, there are a number who will also suffer physical violence. The Narcissist uses physical aggression and force to get their victims to comply. This can include physical rages of erupting actions like being hit, kicked, slapped, punched, strangled, throttled, burned, choked, shoved or having objects thrown at them, are just some examples. The assault is deliberate and is there to demonstrate the abusers power, control and dominance over the victim.

Any act of bodily harm, which leaves, bruises, marks, broken bones, injury or trauma physically. Threats of violence can occur throughout the relationship to keep you in your place as a warning of what will happen if your abuser perceives that you have stepped out of line in someway in their warped minds. Making statements such as "if you do that again, you'll be sorry" or "why do you provoke me, you know what happens when I get mad".

They are designed to keep you imprisoned and living in a constant state of fear. Sometimes they may start off with verbal threats, which can turn into physical acts of abuse. Once the abuser has physically hurt you, lashed out and caused significant harm they may very well turn back on their fake charm and apologise for their outbursts or continue to blame you for causing them to react in this abusive manner in the first place.

Then things might start to simmer down over the next couple of days, weeks until the anger manifests and bubbles up once again and the whole cycle is re-enacted. Usually when the physical abuser can't lash out in public they will stick to emotional abuse. Normally, physical abuse goes on behind closed doors in secret. It can leave victims in fear of their lives, but yet too scared to leave in case the abuser tries to stop them and ultimately even kill them in some extreme cases. By threatening and intimidating the victim they demand unquestioned obedience and compliance. The harsh act of physical abuse is a punishment the perpetrator feels entitled to carry out with no fear of consequences or genuine remorse. They have a bottomless pit of fury and poor impulse control.

From my own experience I endured bouts of physical contact from being shoved to throttled, even kicked in bed at times scattered throughout my marriage and even being pushed so hard against a wall once while pregnant. As soon as the abuse ended I would see my ex Narcissist fall to the ground on his hands and knees begging for forgiveness while I listened on to fake insincere apologies of how it would never happen again. I reasoned and justified to myself it wasn't that bad, or he was sorry it wouldn't happen again and shockingly I explained to myself it wasn't that serious as he hadn't punched me or left any physical bruises so therefore it wasn't domestic violence like I had seen in the news or movies.

Sometimes the abuse in toxic relationships can start off gradually such as with a shove or a push here or there and then get progressively worse over time. Victims may feel trapped, alone and afraid of their partner.

They are so worn down and on tender hooks not knowing when or what will trigger or cause another explosive encounter.

They may avoid certain topics or actions in order to try to appease them and also try to predict their outbursts to avoid them in the future.

The abusers violent behaviour is never acceptable and is always their responsibility, the same as when they're using their other abusive tactics. They are an aggressive bully who acts violently to scare you into submission by resorting to physical abuse. The only response from you should be to make an escape plan and get the hell out of there and protect yourself and children if you have any.

# Chapter 18

# Passive/Aggressive Behaviour-

Passive/aggressive behaviour may come across as accidental or random but it is actually intentional deliberate behaviour veiled as subtle comments and insults causing confusion, bending the facts and distorting reality. It makes a situation harder to judge and recognise whether what you see or hear is in its true form. It can be a compliment given to you, which is actually underhanded and meant as an insult in disguise. It can be an action that at first glance is a nice gesture but once taken a closer look at, is a backhanded swipe at you.

Their words and actions never match up. They are misplaced and disjointed. Your abuser may say something like "you look lovely tonight, *but* you would've looked even better if you had worn the black dress". Or say it's your birthday and you're going out for dinner. They may book an expensive restaurant to celebrate but when it's time to leave, they drag it out and suddenly make up an excuse e.g. say they've got an important phone call to make, so you're left frustrated and late for your own special meal. If your driving they might physically gesture holding onto their seat belt extra tight or by gripping the side handle to imply your driving is dangerous and unsteady whilst at the same time saying your a good driver, this in turn unsettles you eroding your confidence and self esteem. By covertly undermining your driving, you question your ability even if your the best driver in the world, the abuser will subtly suggest your incapable and you will end up doubting yourself and driving skills. Each time this is repeated until you don't feel confident anymore and you may end up letting the abuser take over the driving altogether, which was their plan all along to gain more control over you and another tactic to takeaway your independence.

Other times they build you up and then leave deliberate hints and gestures to bring you down or ruin special occasions etc. These covert tactics are an indirect way of showing aggression but dressing them up in a fanciful embellished way. It's designed to upset, frustrate, confuse the other person whilst being covered and hidden from sight. It's a sneaky behaviour where the culprit isn't so easy to recognise. The hidden abuse is concealed with pleasant interactions in agreement by being polite and friendly but with a negative under tone and connotation, their words are riddled with cryptic messages and evasive meaning.

# Chapter 19

## *Hot/Cold Behaviour-*

One way to spot you are dating a Narcissist or an unhealthy individual is when they play the hot/cold games. These are cycles of where they shower you with doses of hot behaviour such as love, attention, compliments, flattery and give you warmth and affection. Then their behaviour gets erratic and just like a switch they then start to blow cold like the wind. They become distant and emotionally silent. Aloof and icy. I also call these mixed signals part of their push/pull dance. By withdrawing they are keeping you locked in a confused state of frustration and exhaustion. You will probably try harder to communicate and get back some affection or even some kind of pleasant acknowledgement at least.

Desperately you want to engage in the loving and caring behaviour that they over the top showered you with in the beginning. After them pulling away and being subjected to their cold indifference, which could vary from minutes to hours to days, to the tides then turning and being injected with sparse signs of the love and affection once again; you will be subjected to a similar watered-down version of the love bombing stage.

In turn as you begin to minimise and excuse away the first bouts of strange cold behaviour, you start to get comfortable lapping up some warmth and attention, enjoying soaking up the glorious suns rays once again.

Although it doesnt last long as it feels like you've stayed out in the sun far too long as your suddenly scalded and burned and the rug is then pulled from underneath you and guess what- Mr/Mrs Hyde is back. The fun, charming, kind and caring Dr Jekyll has vanished and once again you are back on the merry-go-round of madness, confusion and insecurity. His/her inconsistency and your emotions will swing like a constant pendulum. This predictable pattern will oscillate between the two extremes of being *adored* to *ignored*. Swinging back and forth, from their fake charm to their toxic manipulation can leave you stuck, hanging in midair, not knowing whether you are coming or going, feeling insecure, unsafe and uncertain. Their drips of affection keep us from leaving and wanting desperately for Dr Jekyll to stay for good hoping for him/her to return each time as a permanent fixture. In the end, all you do is live on the edge of hope. Every now and then you will get glimpses of the nice guy/girl act, just enough to keep you hooked.

The reasons for this shift in extremes is to slowly train you to be dependent on the Narcissist and to comply to their demanding commands. Just like the silent treatment they can use these tactics as a form of punishment. Another reason is as they become bored so easily they are always on the lookout for new shiny supply. Their warped little heads are on constant pivot, poaching out fresh new prey. The times when they are blowing cold on you, are the times they are fixated on another, giving and getting attention from different sources. You alone cannot provide them with their insatiable need of constant fuel. Therefore, by devaluing you they are receiving negative fuel from your painful reactions, whilst also at the same time, gaining an extra helping of new positive fuel elsewhere. The natural normal response from the victim is to question 'why is my partner withdrawing'?, 'why are they ignoring me'?

So, you start to cling looking for answers and the more you cling, the more the Narcissist pulls away, calling you more degrading names and accusing you of being far too sensitive or needy. They persuade you that once again your normal human reactions are somehow wrong and you're the one at fault for questioning their behaviour and the one acting unreasonable. It is mind-boggling and insane to watch how a Narcissist can switch on and off these two personas and then on top twist everything around into being your fault. The victim tries harder to salvage what has been lost and wants to save the emotional investment they have put in. Therefore, they tend to stay and get trapped on the rollercoaster of doom.

The continuous pattern of receiving just enough crumbs to keep you locked in the game. Even if the victim musters up enough courage to put an end to this madness and tries to set a boundary or ultimatum and walk away, the Narcissist will go back into full-blown pursuit mode and use their manipulation skills to ensnare you back into their evil clutches. If you are weak, have doubts about leaving and succumb, you may think you've taught them a lesson as you begin once again to lap up the excessively caring and attentive partner they promise to be once again. Unfortunately for those who have been in toxic relationships or with Narcissists know full well this is short lived and their confident loving veneer begins to melt away once again. It's a repetitive cycle, which is part of their dysfunctional personality disorder.

# Chapter 20

# Why you're Addicted to the Narcissist?

The Narcissist is a professional performer who knows that playing their push and pull games, it leads the victim to an addiction of receiving the extreme highs and lows. From the very beginning you were consumed with feelings of euphoria due to the intense 'love bombing', then trained over time to experience intoxicating peaks and unbelievable torturous valleys. We crave love and it stimulates the same addictive neurological pathways as amphetamines. We are trained to be addicted to this reward system.

The powerful surge of dopamines you experience in their presence is a catalyst to stay fixated on these recurrent highs. This is the addiction process – the loving feeling changes your mood – by engaging with the Narcissist and stimulating your reward system, then even with the negative drama you can't stop. The intermittent thrill is all you end up chasing. By the Narcissist lowering your expectations and throwing you some crumbs every now and then, it is the intermittent reinforcement, which overrides your logical brain function and you live for those emotional waves of mania and thrills of excitement.

The psychological addiction drives our compulsions wanting 'more', and this in turn overrides pain, fear and self-respect. Even when you know in your head that the relationship is wrong and damaging to yourself, when you're separated from your partner your award centre still craves the closeness and an unhealthy obsession to stay connected with your abuser can be overpowering. A similar pattern is when people gamble. You may put £10 in a fruit machine and then win say £20 back, thus making a profit of £10. This thrill and adrenaline rush triggers you to try again thinking to oneself, maybe if I keep going I can win the jackpot! So the more you play, the more hooked you are at chasing the 'Golden win'.

At times you may lose and at other times you may win, even though over all the odds are stacked against you and your forever chasing the carrot on the end of the stick – setting yourself up for failure due to the unpredictable random reward system.

Unfortunatly, the same addiction takes place in romantic toxic relationships. When not knowing if or when the big win arises (love, affection, validation will resume) it makes the partnership much more exciting and intoxicating. The constant feelings of hit or miss are very addictive. At times your abuser acts loving, caring and praises you and at other times thrown in for good measure, they ignore you becoming withdrawn and distant making you feel like you have to 'work harder' to gain back their attention and love.

Another reason for the powerful attachment you are experiencing has been created by our biochemical bonds. When rejected in a relationship you feel hurt and experience pain literally as your brain is wired to share the same circuitry system, which mirrors that as physical pain. This area of the brain lights up when you are hurt physically and it is the same area that lights up when your hurt and suffer emotionally.

A mixed chain of powerful chemicals in your brain make a cocktail of addictive behaviours and unhealthy attachment bonds.

- *Dopamine*- which controls the pleasure part of our brains

- *Oxytocin*- which is through the power of touch, named the "love or cuddle" hormone

- *Cortisol*- regulates our reactions to stressful situations and ignites a 'fight or flight' response

- *Adrenaline*- is released in response to a stressful, exciting, dangerous or threatening situation

- *Serotonin* - this regulates and stabilises your mood, but when in toxic relationships levels of serotonin drops and can cause our rational decision-making abilities and judgement to go out of the window

- *Trauma bonds*- The fear and pleasure are entwined and create an adverse deep bond between you and the abuser- which means even when someone you feel so close to and love, hurts you, you experience what's called 'trauma bonding'. Trauma bonds create and seal intense feelings with shared experiences that you've spent with the abuser.

*Exploring in more detail the above biochemicals on why our bodies become addicted to abusive partners like a drug.*

**Dopamine** is the neurotransmitter, which is responsible for certain drug addictions such as cocaine. It hits the pleasure zone and creates attention, wanting, drive, motivation and anticipation of reward.

It reacts in the same way to romantic partnerships. In both instances of using certain drugs or being in an intense relationship with a Narcissist the pleasurable memories trigger Dopamine, which creates these reward circuits in the brain, that I mentioned earlier. These continue to play a repetitive loop that keeps going around in your mind and then gets stuck in a dangerous cycle.

**Oxytocin** is responsible for the addictive bonding with your abuser and is known as the "love hormone". It plays a powerful role in social and bonding relationships and also sexual reproduction. In healthy relationships it is a great chemical to give off a strong sense of connection and creates a bond of trust. Unfortunately it is deadly in toxic relationships even if you know your partner is a bad match for you, due to the 'Love drug' you get hooked and it's a hard addiction to break. It basically creates a false bond of trust between you and your abuser.

**Cortisol** is known as the "stress hormone". In toxic relationships it is released when responding to a fearful or stressful situation. It comes from the adrenal glands and is part of the (3 f's) **FIGHT / FLIGHT/ FREEZE** mechanisms. When exposed to stressful events the cortisol levels jump up and can affect your heart rate, digestion and mind. You may react to an imminent threat of danger by running away from the situation **Flight** or by staying and faceing it and want to **Fight**. The **Fight** response is to outfight our attackers and **Flight** is to outrun them, to get away far as possible to a place of safety. Both are defense mechanisms about survival in hostile predicaments. It warns us there's danger and switches on our internal alert panic button. Either way by experiencing high levels of cortisol in your body it has a negative impact on your health and well being in the long-term.

Sometimes in dysfunctional toxic relationships when we are not fleeing or fighting our abuser, the rest of the time we tend to go into denial mode, bury our heads in the sand and **FREEZE** like a deer in the headlights, as a reaction to being in a traumatic environment. Our **Freeze** response occurs when we give up hope and accept the situation for what it is and try to make the best of it, especially when feeling like there is no chance to fight back or escape. It overwhelms you and leaves you mentally paralyzed in a state of fear and helplessness. It blocks out the true harrowing enormity of abuse and what's really happening to you.

The mind freezes and you begin to dissociate from your reality and situation as another method of coping and a self-defence mechanism. Our instincts are taken over by the above (3 f's) and determine which one will primarily be your response in a stressful situation. All three are aimed to protect ourselves.

**Adrenaline** is a stimulant and stimulants are addictive. It is a hormone also produced by the adrenal glands plus some neurons and plays an important role in the Fight/Flight responses as mentioned above. It increases blood flow around the body and will make your heart race, your hands sweat and puts you on high alert ready to respond. This combined with the hormone Cortisol, pumps you up to go into battle head on or to run away and escape. Persistent high levels of **Adrenaline** from long term stress can make you more likely to develop and experience heart disease, anxiety and depression.

You may also stay due to **Conditioning** which is a learned response developed by experiencing repetitive behaviour; victims learn to perform and act in certain ways through a reward or punishment system that follows the behaviour. It is training the victims cognitive abilities by using a range of tactics including positive reinforcement e.g. (praise, affection, turning on the superficial charm once again, gifts, fake flattery) against bouts of opposing tactics such as negative reinforcement e.g. (aggressive tone of voice, facial expressions of disapproval, guilt trips, silent treatments, rages, intimidation). This conditioning is based on an alternation swinging between loving behaviour followed by abusive behaviour. The victim becomes so confused by the ever-changing positive/negative behaviours that they start to accept this see-saw treatment and the negative projections become incorporated in their self-image. They become reliant and focused on pacifying the Narcissist, trying desperately to regain the love and positive behaviour of the abuser.

They are always testing and violating your boundaries, pushing your tolerance and limits further and further while you struggle and scurry to please the Narcissist and stay in their good books anticipating the next time you are basking in their light. You are tied to your abuser by invisible chains. Even though the front door is unlocked you are frozen and too emotionally bonded to the Narcissist, unable and unwilling to open the door and walk away. You feel powerless and out of fear you stay. You are scared of the unknown, uncertainty and being alone.

On top of this you may develop **Stockholm Syndrome.** It is a condition that causes victims to develop a psychological attachment, a union with their abusers as a survival strategy during trauma and abuse. These strong emotional ties develop after intimate and on-going abuse. The trauma creates a dependent bond to the abuser especially when they have snippets of acts of kindness in between the obvious abuse displayed. The term Stockholm syndrome, was introduced in 1973- when during a bank robbery in Stockholm, Sweden, four hostages were taken. These hostages had been so traumatised and brainwashed that they actually defended their captors after being released and would not agree to testify in court against them. The survivors have a paradoxical experience of self-contradicting and irrational feelings and thoughts.

Any rational person from the outside would feel utter contempt and disgust towards the captors. But not so for the hostages, they have the opposite viewpoint and see their perpetrators in a good light and want to protect and defend them even after all their cruelty. It is exactly the same reaction created between the Narcissist and the victim. You end up becoming submissive, normalising and rationalising the bad treatment to cope and survive in a physiological war-zone. It can be one of our defence mechanisms to create a delusional positive association and bond to our abusers in order to be able to live through the bewildering and incomprehensible adversity and horrific crimes we are subjected to.

# Chapter 21

# Why do you keep repeating the same patterns and attracting toxic partners?

Subconsciously, we are drawn to recreate familiar unconscious comfortable situations and emotional exchanges that we experienced as children. Even if we experienced an unhealthy or hostile childhood, we still unknowingly may attract and reenact the same dynamics as an adult. As adults we have to consciously realise we are not helpless children any more and we need to ask ourselves what life is trying to teach us and to become aware that now we have the power and choices to control our present and stop the negative re-occurring toxic patterns by shining light on them, exposing them and making a conscious choice of self-protection, wellbeing and pure love.

We can only truly love, when we are free and let go of fear. We tend to carry these unconscious and unhealed fears such as rejection/ abandonment or engulfment into our primary relationships.

As children growing up we may have been exposed to toxic environments and maybe even having parents or siblings who were Narcissistic. This then sets the precedent for how we view the world and in a sick way as adults strangely only feel comfortable, familiar and safe involved with other abusers as an adult. This overwhelming conditioning is integrated pretty deeply and we are subconsciously carrying out actions and dynamics and learned negative repetitive habits, which we continue to carry out automatically. We pursue deeply embedded beliefs and continue the toxic narrative even if that just means changing the characters and scenery. We can be drawn to the same abusive characteristics, traits and scenarios due to not knowing any different. By not knowing what a healthy, loving and calm relationship looks or feels like it is then difficult to realise or wake up that things can be different, there are healthy choices and options out there. Change and edging into unfamiliar territory can be a good thing. Coming from a background of abuse and then going into a healthy relationship at first may feel very foreign and scary, suddenly receiving respect and love for the first time in your life you may not feel worthy of it.

You may be conditioned as a co-dependent and accustomed to always putting other people's needs and wants before your own. You naturally fall into the trap of a people pleaser and automatically ignore your own needs and desires. You can easily be guilt tripped or used as an scapegoat for other people's bad behaviour. You end up supporting, enabling the abuser and becoming reliant and dependent on them in return for approval and a sense of identity. Your over the top sacrificial actions weave you into a web of toxic pollution, which has harmful and poisonous effects. You willingly accept and take responsibility for others dysfunctional actions and can naturally end up in intimate relationships with the primary role of carer, rescuer or saviour. As a co-dependent you put the abusers needs as a priority and yours at the bottom of the pecking order. You depend on your perpetrators love and approval for internal fulfilment. You are a perfect match and pairing for someone with a Personality Disorder who in turn is also a co-dependent. Their motivation and function is purely to get their needs met and they solely depend and rely on empathetic and good natured caring people to fill them up, as they cannot self regulate happy content emotions or feelings on their own. This is why you may keep being drawn to Narcissists as you both follow the *co-dependent dance.* The co-dependent victim naturally takes role of caregiver and nurturer and the abuser co-dependent naturally takes the role of selfish, self-absorbed demanding controller. The victim is looking to depend, feel needed and wanted and the abuser seeks victims who put other people's needs before their own. This match suits both individuals unconscious needs in a toxic dysfunctional manner.

I know myself I was very codependent and at 17 I didn't have an individual identity yet so I went into caretaker mode and put my abuser above my own needs and wants as he was my identity. My whole life was wrapped up around him. Every thought, action or feeling would revolve around my Narcissist. How the things I did, said or acted and behaved would affect him. I was also very naturally an empathic and compassionate person who wanted to save/fix him the minute I met him, feeling overwhelmingly responsible similar to protecting and saving an injured bird. I lapped up his sob story of coming from a broken family, where his Dad was an alcoholic who physically assaulted and abused him and his mother growing up and he was accustomed to experiencing a turbulent unstable life in and out of domestic violence shelters. I could see the scared little boy beneath his adult body and felt obliged and drawn to fully invest and sacrifice myself and life to help and become his saviour.

Of course by repressing and ignoring my own self throughout the years was a perfect fit for my (never ending) demanding and insatiable Narcissist. The cycle was a compulsive addiction and I felt comfortable in that role of forever chasing trying to fix, change and heal another person, while I slowly evaporated into the shadows and became a slave all in the name of love. My intentions were good but taking on a martyr's role was always going to be self-defeating, self harming and self-destructive. After a lot of heartache and self-discovery I now know you can never change or control another person. You can only change yourself. You can only control your own actions and reactions to events in life. No matter how good and sincere your intent is for another, we are all on our own journey and path and must take responsibility and accountability for our own actions, behaviour and part. It is not our job to fill someone who is empty and lost. It is not our job to sacrifice ourselves for another. We have to establish our own sense of self and know when others are taking advantage of us and when our over the top caregiving becomes harmful to our well-being.

By being conditioned to the bad treatment you experienced and maybe having no choice to leave, you end up instead being psychologically imprisoned to stay, accepting the situation and thus getting into a habit of learned helplessness. It occurs when you're exposed to chronic negative situations and you feel helpless. It's your personal belief that you are incapable of escaping your current situation so you instead just give up and surrender. Instead of battling back (**fight**) or fleeing (**flight**) you submit (**freeze**), paralysed in a state of self helplessness where you feel you have no control over your choices or surroundings. Victims can remain stationary and passive despite their clear ability to change their situation. It's a point of totally giving up and handing over your free will to your abuser. People on the outside might wonder if a person is being abused, then why don't they leave?
They are an adult so why are they putting up with unacceptable harmful behaviour and staying?

**It's like being trapped in a cage yet the door is wide open.**

By the victims identity slowly being chipped away, they ultimately take away your self-esteem and confidence. You are left feeling weak and leaves you incapable to make even the simplest of decisions on your own, making you even more dependent on your abuser and too stuck, scared to leave for the fear of change and uncertainty.

Many people don't realise that it's extremely difficult to leave a toxic abusive relationship. As with learned helplessness it's not always about physical harm but mental power over the victim. The perpetrators goal is to wear the victim down so much and take away any personal power and freedom they once had. The victim resigns themselves into believing that change and getting help is harder and impossible to access and implement than staying and instead willingly accept abuse as now part of their expectations and their life.

As an adult you may believe you only deserve toxic people and negativity. You might believe that you deserve bad treatment as you don't feel worthy or valuable enough for anything more. These feelings, beliefs and misconceptions are once again shaped and driven by our early childhood experiences. Growing up in a dysfunctional and unstable drama infested home can be a blueprint of what's to come. You may automatically be drawn to commotion and turbulence as an adult and excuse abuse instead for intense love and excitement. Thus in turn shunning healthy calm stable relationships, labelling them as boring and dull. You imagine and experience them as being unstimulating and bland, colourless and passionless. Instead you thrive and are drawn to powerful explosive exhilarating and unpredictable relations.

Practicing inner self-work on myself I discovered and unburied the reasons why I think I was drawn to a Narcissistic partner and stayed for so many years. There can be lots of components for the reasons why we get into these types of toxic relationships and stay. Including valid common reasons such as commitment, investment or financial reasons, especially once children are involved. Not to mention being hooked by the trauma bonds and biochemicals, which keep us stuck. When I explored further, I suspect I was also drawn into the inevitable highs and lows of a relationship with a Narcissist because as a child growing up with my Mum who was clinically diagnosed with manic depression (now known as bi-polar disorder). Looking back at my childhood it was surrounded by these eloping and fleeting experiences. I was exposed and conditioned to living with my main caregiver who was at times emotionally unavailable, unstable and uncertain. I always knew my Mum loved me and she always did her best even working nights as a nurse to put me through private school, but it was hard growing up watching her emotions swing from one mood to another erratically. The worst time I remember was when my Mum was sectioned for having an out of control episode. I went to visit her in the Priory in London as a teenager and I remember she was so out of this world and in a bad place, she barely recognised me. That was the toughest thing to see my once happy loving parent suddenly turn into a lost, depressed, zombie state and become an incapable person. I suppose I was confused at times and her illness hard to comprehend. Although I was lucky my Dad was a Doctor, he was also a loving and supporting husband and father, who could individually cope and explain to me the reasons for my Mums dark illness. This in turn helped me to cope the best I could growing up in an unpredictable childhood. Reflecting further it put my Dad in a position of complete dominance as he had no choice but to take over the roles of two parents, work, look after me and my brother whilst my Mum was in hospital. I saw a strong powerful male influence who I suppose came across at times as controlling in order to keep the boat afloat and I was dependent on these dynamics. Therefore in turn unconsciously, I was probably drawn and attracted to these strong confident qualities in my Narcissistic partner.

Once time had passed and my Mum was put on the correct medication and had the invaluable treatment she needed to get better, I had my Mum back. Although it wasn't always smooth sailing as her moods could still go up or down, life gradually balanced out and became familiar and normalised once again. I can now logically understand and see how being in a turbulent adult relationship mimicked and felt familiar, comfortable to me. The dynamics were eerily similar at times and maybe unconsciously I wanted to help my partner/abuser get better and get the help they needed to change just like my mother got her help. Unfortunately a mental illness like my Mothers is not the same or even treatable as a personality disorder. They may mimic similar qualities and characteristics, but a mental disorder is a chemical imbalance which can be regulated and treated thankfully with strong drugs. Anyone with a Personality Disorder has a character flaw and it is ingrained in them as children, which is part of their make up and defence mechanisms so no drugs can fix this ongoing chronic problem.

It is important for you all to go on your own journey of deep self-discovery and tap into your awareness and consciousness of why you think you may keep attracting toxic partners. Only you know the answer to that question and only you can do the work needed to avoid/repel the same dysfunctional patterns moving forward. Instead, by changing your belief systems and negative programming, you can evolve, grow and attract and enjoy a caring healthy respectful mutual partnership in the future.

# Chapter 22

# Triangulation and Harem's-

To continually gain the upper hand, keep victims off balance and always second-guessing themselves a Narcissist enjoys the game of *triangulation*.

By introducing a third person into the dynamics when in a relationship or even when it is ending or ended. The purpose is to create more drama, doubt and mental anguish in the victim. The third person could be a work colleague, mutual friend, family member, acquaintance, ex-lover and even future supply. Usually they use the opposite sex to cause confusion, jealousy and insecurity. It is a red beacon hanging over the relationship warning you that they are always in demand, there's always a chance that you can be replaced any moment, the Narcissist is desirable and constantly has other options if you should dare misbehave or not comply. It is a constant lingering threat underpinning your toxic relationship that creates an illusion of superiority, alluring appeal and attractiveness in the Narcissist.

Naturally, it elevates the abuser into a higher position of value, worth and produces a misleading impression of reality. The victim in turn will always feel uncertain, on edge, balancing on eggshells trying to appease and try harder not to do anything wrong, to rock the boat or upset them, as they ultimately don't want to lose the Narcissist and this fear carries them through the entire relationship. There is no balance, security or stability. No genuine reassurance that you would find in a normal healthy partnership. By manufacturing the toxic triangle the Narcissist loves the attention and admiration from both parties involved. They thrive off of the power, reactions, and conflict orchestrating a spectacle and pulling the strings of all the people involved. The Narcissist has an ability to pit people against each other, to enter an unknown competition to compete for a place in their lives for affection and acknowledgement. The triangulation is a manipulation technique where the perpetrator will secretly discuss and communicate with supporters and yes people behind the victims back. By ultimately controlling and manoeuvering communication the Narcissist is in charge of what dialogue gets back to which individuals. They influence opinions, situations and outcomes to their advantage.

*A common example of this is using an upside down triangle.*

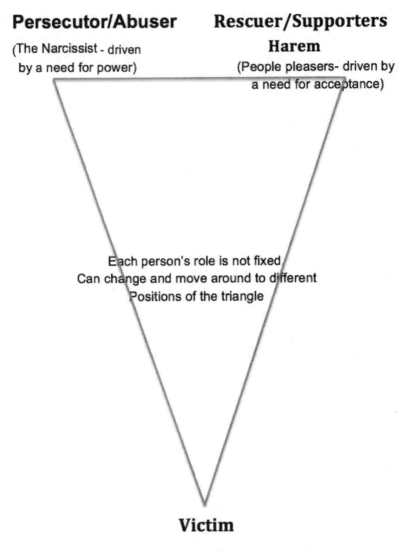

**Persecutor/Abuser**

(The Narcissist - driven
by a need for power)

**Rescuer/Supporters**
**Harem**

(People pleasers- driven by
a need for acceptance)

Each person's role is not fixed
Can change and move around to different
Positions of the triangle

**Victim**

(Kind empathetic- driven by a need
for a purpose and as a place of belonging,
fall into the trap as they don't have their
own identity)

In the beginning you would of taken pride of place as **rescuer** for the poor wounded Narcissist, who would have portrayed themselves as the **victim** from their evil ex (the false **perpetrator**).

Over time these dynamics will change when the Narcissist is bored with you and you'll fall into the devaluation cycle where they will then make you out to be the abuser (top left of the triangle). Convincing you and everyone else that they are once again the victim in this volatile partnership.

You started off as the rescuer, an angel to put the Narcissist back together and to help save them from their horrible ex. This stage would've been in the beginning of the love bombing cycle where you were put on a pedestal and could do no wrong. Unfortunately in reality overtime you are devalued – dropped like a hot potato to the bottom of the triangle and stuck in position of injured party- the victim role. The Narcissists Harem/cheerleaders or new supply is now honoured to hold the title of rescuer and could ultimately be your replacement. The true fixed position of the Narcissist has always been in the top left corner of the triangle as the **abuser** and **perpetrator**. They just created an illusion of moving from this position to victim to gain sympathy and be in a better position to manipulate and deceive.

On top of creating jealousy and confusion, another aim of triangulation is to pit the two people against each other, so that it puts the Narcissist in a good light. The one in the middle who is there to comfort you when you've been isolated and been told lies by the abuser that the third-party has been saying bad words about your character and your intentions behind your back. This dynamic kills two birds with one stone as the abuser uses this manipulation vice versa and tells the other person in the triangle similar things about you insulting and making disrespectful comments about the third-party, which will be useful down the line to further get them on their side. As the Narcissist is the one in the middle creating these complex lies and conflicts they are in charge and control of what is said, what messages get across and are able to get away with planting seeds of animosity, friction and hostility without any detection.

They are the puppeteer and messenger in the centre so whatever situation they create or words they tell you, in turn make you naturally lean on them becoming reliant and dependent. Of course the Narcissist will do their best to keep you furthest apart from the third-party and vice versa as otherwise if you get too close, interact and exchange direct communication you may find out all the outrageous lies and tricks the Narcissist has falsely created. They don't want any chance of detection or exposure so by saying bad stuff about each other you unintentionally are more trusting and believe the Narcissist and naturally avoid the person they're telling lies about.

The Narcissist excels at pretending they are actually just protecting you from the third party, when in reality they are just isolating you further, destroying your reputation and enjoying slagging you off behind your back, making you out to be the crazy insane one. By doing so not only is the Narcissist gaining power and leverage over you but they are purposefully setting the future stage, ready for when you fall from grace. As by planting the seeds early on in their harems minds, it makes the process easier and smoother for them when it comes to discarding you. It will come as no shock or surprise to the other individuals they have confided in and pitted you off against. Instead they will just think how brave and loyal the Narcissist was to put up with you for all those weeks, months or years. You will automatically be made out to be the bad person due to the false manufactured information which was suggested over the course of your devaluation. So, not only will you be belittled and devalued overtly to your face but also betrayed, stabbed in the back by the one you thought was your loving partner. By getting others on their side it backs up and reinforces the Narcissists continuous fake lies and accusations as well as fuelling extra support and ammo against the victim.

Not only will a Narcissist be disrespectful and create lies and conflict between you and a third party but also have other deluded and misinformed supporters, cheerleaders and disciples in the background called *"Harems"*. These are a group of individuals who gravitate and centre around the Narcissist at any opportunity. They are always there to take the Narcissists side automatically and champion them so the victim feels undermined, attacked and ganged up on.

By the Narcissist having this fanclub in the shadows they know they always have options no matter what. The harem is a selection of admirers of the opposite sex or people pleasers. Having either been used by the Narcissist before many times, ex partners who ended up getting the friendship card after being used and abused and now dumped on the harem pile for future use, or new shiny future supply waiting in the wings who is clueless and doesn't yet know anything about the Narcissists games and true-self.

Jealousy is a very powerful emotion and by either subtly or obviously parading these females/males in your direction, you will constantly be made to feel under threat, undermined and uncertain where you stand in the relationship. They are there to boost the Narcissist's ego and to be a constant source of attention and supply whenever they get bored with you to fall back on or to use them in their triangulation and manipulation games. Most members of the harem are unsuspecting and don't realise that there are others in the group. The Narcissist will tell them all the same lies and promises to give them hope that they could have a chance with the Narcissist any time, just by telling them what they want to hear, whispering sweet nothings to keep them on tap. One way or another the harem's expectations have been so broken down and are just left hanging on for some type of validation, approval anything to feel like they belong somewhere and to be part of something. By the Narcissist giving them crumbs they continue to hang on. Even if it means being second, fifth or tenth in the hierarchy, it doesn't matter as belonging somewhere is better than nothing. Instead of cutting all ties with the Narcissist, realising their own worth and moving forward with a partner where a stable healthy relationship is possible, they stay as a member, always an option never a priority, waiting in the shadows to be used and exploited further. You may also find other dysfunctional unhealthy females/males in their harem who have nothing better to do than to gain fuel off of watching and participating and hurting others. This involvement and inclusion makes them feel like they have some kind of special bond with the Narcissist and that they can carry out their twisted games together.

I call these modern day harems– *"minions"*. They are just like honey bees who are working for the Queen bee in a colony, dutiful drones performing specialised tasks, serving, defending and protecting, just as the minions do the same for the Narcissist.

Certain members can also be the same sex, weaved into the mix of brothers, sisters, family members, old school friends even strangers which add to the weight of the Harem to falsely support the Narcissist. Social media is a great tool for Narcissists to use these followers, minions and collect people to do their bidding. It is another platform to use, manipulate and gain unrelenting likes and attention from their 'Fanclub'. They are an advocate to champion the Narcissist if they are feeling down, need an ego stroke or someone to play rivalry games with.

The harem can be as big as the Narcissist likes and is a constant reassurance of how great and mighty they are. Whether a harem member is aware of it or not, they are supporting and adding to their already over inflated ego. A constant supply of online supporters do not know everything about the Narcissist, their agenda or intentions but only what the Narcissist posts and wants them to see. So sometimes harems can unintentionally back up the Narcissist as they only see one side of the coin, which is the confident, happy, go lucky or poor misunderstood respected guy/girl. Remember using social media you can portray yourself into whatever image you want others to see and believe in. You can easily hide your bad bits, flaws and dysfunction.

So the Narcissist knows they will always be seen in a good light and have the harem agree with all their issues and problems as they don't really know the half of it. Their members tell them exactly what they want to hear, without knowing all the facts. The Narcissist thrives off this, as they need people to survive. The harem is a Narcissist's oxygen tank, designed to be in constant flow and maintained regularly and topped up when getting low. If attention from the primary source starts declining, then they will always have this backup supply in reserve.

They need as many options and superficial people as possible. They don't care how many people they hurt or use in the process as inevitably casualties are of no concern. Only generating a constant 'buzz' of supply of validation around the Narcissist is of importance to them. They need the outside world to feed their excessive demands and confirm their deluded grandiose false sense of self.

# Chapter 23

# Smear Campaign/Revenge-

During the aftermath of destruction and heartbreak for the victim, once discarded it is emphasised even more by the cruel Narcissist enjoying the new game of the fallout and after-effects to continue to gain supply. Unfortunately, even once you're thrown away on the scrapheap, disposed of- the war isn't yet over. For now the abuser has the perfect opportunity to rub salt in your open wounds and further discredit and damage your well-being, reputation and support networks.

This tactic is called the *smear campaign,* which is an intentional move to create further trauma for the victim. It is designed to additionally destroy your credibility and character and paint you as the unhinged crazy abuser. You're the unfortunate target of their calculating crusade and they act out shamelessly by retaliating and seeking *revenge.*

Revengeful for what? You may ask yourself, when you've done no apparent wrong. The only wrongdoing you did was by hanging around far too long, believing their web of lies, falling for their broken promises and investing so much into something that was inevitably futile. To a Narcissist all your good kindness, loyalty and genuine support, intentions and positivity go out of the window.

It is meaningless to them as one way or another you are scorned and have given them a Narcissistic injury whether real or perceived. They go full out to bring you further face down in the mud and punish you for barely breathing.

Whether you ended the relationship or they did is of no relevance, as either way you will be punished for either rejecting or challenging them or due to the fact that a lot of them are sadists. They enjoy the power and control of further isolating you, discrediting you and ultimately spinning your world upside down and trying to turn loved ones, friends and family against you. It is the icing on the cake for a malignant Narcissist to watch you slowly sink further down into anxiety and depression while gleefully gloating as you struggle to defend yourself aimlessly. They are cold and robotic in their approach and ruthless in giving no consideration or care to your feelings or history together. Having no moral compass, a missing empathy chip and being emotionally bankrupt makes their slandering and tarnishing of you all the more easy. Masters at undermining you, telling lies and half truths, distorting reality is their expertise craft. They will callously spread rumours and invent malicious twisted tales. This is also due to the fact that they are lacking object consistency. So instead they see others as either being black or white, good or bad, a hero or an enemy. They struggle to understand that human beings are three-dimensional people, a mixture of good and bad qualities, with a combination of tastes and preferences and different opinions and ideas than those of their own.

On the other hand, normal individuals and healthy formed relationships have whole object relations, which means they can understand and accept that people are not always perfect yet at the same time still value that person and appreciate the good qualities and characteristics, which outweigh the negative. Healthy individuals can maintain a positive emotional connection to someone they care and love, even when maybe that person has upset them and is possibly feeling frustrated or angry. It is being able to see the bigger picture and demonstrating what unconditional love is. Having a mature and compassionate insight to both parties. Narcissists on the other hand either see you as a rescuer/angel or as their enemy/competitor who is out to get them. There is no in between, there is no balance or strong connection, which would usually solidify two loving people together. You are all or nothing in their dark murky eyes. They are unable to see the real you, the whole puzzle, they literally disassociate from any previous positive feelings and instead only have tunnel vision concentrating only on the bad if you become a perceived threat. That's why in the beginning you were placed on a pedestal, portrayed as amazing and special only to realise you are in fact imperfect (like all humans).

Under this new realisation they feel nothing but disdain and contempt and now need to exterminate you in their abnormal delusional minds. Your name will be dragged through the mud without a backward glance and you will feel like you're being attacked by a pack of hungry wolves. By the Narcissist having already set the scene previously by slandering and devaluing you, the harems and enablers are ready waiting to back up the Narcissist's false claims and join in the invented smear campaign. The Narcissist slips back into victim mode and depicts you as the crazy twisted abuser. Naturally you may feel like you want to lash back out, defend and protect yourself. You desperately want to set the record straight and scream from the rooftops the truth, you were abused, you are a good person who has done no wrong, who is just caught up in a torturous uncontrollable scandal.

You are retraumatised by not only enduring the toxic abuse within the relationship but also the repercussions and backlash of the ending of the union. Just when you are trying to feel some ground underneath your feet again, make sense of everything, picking up the pieces of your shattered heart the abuser has other ideas and skilfully constructs another trap which is waiting for you to get caught back into. They lure, bait and provoke you stirring up your emotions and reactions trying to control the overall outcome. Spinning reality and making accusations via direct dialogue or social media to mutual individuals and groups. Their manufactured self-serving network of minions are an excellent source of secondary supply that further help prop up the Narcissist's false perfect image. They rely on their fanclub to hold the fort and to veil them from being exposed and escape all responsibility and accountability. By assigning hidden roles over to their champions they can then in turn sit back, relax and watch the show unfold right in front of their eyes. Their harem can continue to destroy the already weak defenceless victim. What the Narcissist creates, orchestrates and gets away with is shocking.

These powerful attacks behind the scenes can leave victims feeling even more hopeless, depressed and even suicidal in severe cases. The relentless Narcissist knows their victims weaknesses, vulnerabilities and can play them out and turn them to their advantage in their toxic game. The smear campaign diverts attention away from the real situation and truth and instead focuses negatively on the victim. Putting them in a bad light due to the fact that the problems and lies were implemented and drip fed to the enablers before the break up.

It is very effective and plausible in the Narcissist's favour as the smear campaign is likely to have been going on behind the victims back for weeks or months, which planted the seeds that something was wrong with them, they are unstable, manipulative and the precarious one. So when the abuser decides it's time to discard the victim it is of no surprise to the close people around them. They have been pre-prepped, brainwashed and drip fed lies and false information to inevitably get them on side. These unsuspecting supporters and minions are relieved to hear that the volatile relationship has come to an end and the Narcissist is now free from their horrible ex.

This in turn helps the Narcissist when they publicly parade and flaunt online their new supply. No one bats an eyelid about how swiftly they have moved on, as in their minds they were told about the cracks appearing months ago during the Narcissists smear campaign.

The Narcissist gloats wildly as they show off their new clueless prey. They repeat they tried everything in the old relationship to make it work, but to no avail. It's now time to move on, they deserve happiness and are eager to be the bigger person by walking away. They boast about how happy and content they are with the new catch and praise them vocally for coming into their lives and rescuing them from their crazy ex (you)!

The new *squeeze* is portrayed as the best thing since sliced bread, as you once were. Slotted into your place, taking your sole primary position of girl/boyfriend. Of course, they are none the wiser, innocent and unsuspecting once upon a time like you. Caught up in rescuer mode, lavishing being swept up in the limelight and receiving affection and attention from the false mask. The abuser predictably morphs back into DR Jekyll ready to place the new victim on their mirage pedestal. The Narcissist knows that you will want to justify and defend yourself and in doing so you are playing straight into their hands. That is exactly how they want you to react, as the more vocal you are, the more entangled, defensive and unstable you will frustratingly appear. The more you try to stand up for yourself for your own worth and justice it ends up being counter-productive. The abuser has thoroughly covered all corners for when this scenario arises. It was premeditated and staged precisely to the Narcissists favour and unfair advantage. They were always 10 steps ahead of you. Behind-the-scenes plotting, manoeuvering and conspiring against you. An undercover mole to gain information and intelligence to sabotage and ultimately use against you. They are spurned empty beings who thrive off wreaking havoc and vengeance on unsuspecting victims.

Okay, so you're probably asking yourself what can you do, how can you protect yourself from these lies and false accusations?
You may feel like the more you retaliate and speak up the more it feels like you're losing a grip on reality. Because the smear campaign has been so carefully constructed and convincing, your best bet of shielding yourself from the shrapnel, is by doing and saying 'nothing'. You are ultimately doing the opposite of what the Narcissist expects you to do. You have to make a conscious decision not to engage and participate in any mudslinging matches. By distancing yourself and disengaging the Narcissist loses all power over you. They cannot influence your input and twist anything if you refuse to take part in any more of their outrageous destructive games.

From my own personal experience my Narcissistic ex tried his hardest to provoke and get a reaction out of me after I immediately  found out he was having an affair with one of my old friends (obviously now an ex friend). On top of this I discovered his full deceitfulness and cheating with a number of women, some known to me others were strangers. An example of his childish and despicable behaviour was him using social media as a platform to slag off my character and to continue to parade his new relationship online. The trouble he must've gone to, to create a whole collage of fake loved up poems/photos/quotes etc, desperately boasting how he had met his soulmate and was the happiest he had ever been. Within a few weeks of leaving me, there were pictures of him and her newly engaged (while still married to me). The funny thing is they are a walking contradiction, as to all the enablers and minions he swore down he hadn't cheated, but yet met my friend, fell in love, got engaged within this short period time. On top of this, giving me sexually transmitted diseases but of course still refusing to admit that he had cheated!

That's how absurd it was. But to him it didn't matter he would try any trick in the book to try and provoke me and get me to react. When that failed he then told my daughter aged six about his new wedding plans and showing her pictures of bridesmaid dresses for her!
Just another desperate attempt after being separated for a number of weeks. As you can see from my experience they do not care who they use in their twisted games. My

daughter's emotional well-being was of no concern. Just him staging the next scene for his selfish egotistical self.

Of course, mature healthy adults do not go around causing unnecessary drama, chaos, humiliation, embarrassment and dragging children into the toxic mix when a relationship ends but instead understand that time, respect and consideration for all involved is a priority. This is not normal behaviour but of course common and predictable when dealing with pathological Narcissists. And the answer to your question – no it didn't last.
She was just another prop to use in his manipulation games. Since then he has found new supply, discarded the last one and got enaged once again to a new unaware shiny object to support his fairytale charming fake illusion. This cycle will contiune until his new victim wises up and leaves or they are discarded and once again replaced with another disposable target (people). They will go to any length to get you to engage and triangulate you with the new supply.
Do not fall for their sad, pathetic tournaments.

Now, I'm not saying it's an easy road, as their aim is to turn enough people against you, especially the ones who mean the most. But the individuals who matter will be smart enough to know your character well enough not be fooled by the Narcissist and by biting your tongue, staying calm and grounded, it will give your side more weight. Your close friends and family, the real true people who care and love you who have your best interests at heart, will stick by you. You may lose individuals along the way but then I believe this shows and says more about them than you. They were never a true friend or acquaintance to begin with. Always stay true to yourself. There is nothing wrong with telling people close to you a snippet of your side of things e.g. if they were manipulative, a liar or a cheat. That is fine say your piece and then anything else is out of your control, it's up to others to make up their own minds and come to their own conclusions. It is not your job to force, control or to convince others that you are innocent. This will just further drain you of energy and fuel the fire. Stick to your guns firmly and don't allow the Narcissist to bully and have any hold over you.

By walking away, staying silent speaks volumes about your integrity and character. Do not carry on being a pawn in their game of chess. They will soon get bored and move on to other targets when you choose to disengage and spend your energy elsewhere in a productive and meaningful manner to suit yourself. Dig deep and you will find the strength within you. Become a warrior, trust and have faith that the truth will prevail.

# Chapter 24

## *Hoovering-*

*Hoovering* is a commonly used term in Narcissistic abuse forums and online support communities. It depicts the notion of being sucked back in by the Narcissist once the relationship has ended. Just when you think you have escaped, whether you ended the relationship first or if the Narcissist broke up with you initially and you feel like you're picking up the pieces of your shattered heart and starting to get on with your life, don't get too comfortable. As just when all is quiet and you're starting to feel stronger gaining your sanity back, you may receive a little text out of the blue, a sudden email or even receiving a surprise social media request from your ex Narcissist. Your heart may start to pound, your hands begin to sweat and your head begins to spin again like a shaken martini.

Suddenly your heartstrings start to pull – the confusion mixed with dread, curiosity, hope overwhelm and compel you. Time has passed but their eerie presence is back one way or another. It could be weeks, months or in some cases even years before a Narcissist gets back in touch unexpectedly. Maybe deep down there is a part of you that feels a jump of joy, as you begin to convince yourself maybe they're back as they've changed, they've seen the error of their ways and have missed you so much that they can't live without you. Your wishful thinking continues on autodrive and you assume maybe they realise what a big mistake they have made losing you. Now there is a sign that they want to reconnect and you can finally get your happy ending.

I'm going to **S-T-O-P** you right there in that moment of hopeful, wishful magical thinking and *Snap* you back into reality. For the Narcissist has not changed, they have not suddenly had an epiphany and realised you were the girl/boy of their dreams, nope I hate to break the news to you but you have just been *'Hoovered'*!

The word 'Hoover' is named after the vacuum cleaner, which signals being sucked back into an abusive relationship. Just when you thought you had seen and experienced all their previous dark insidious tricks, this new one hits you like a ton of bricks. It's just another one of their manipulation tactics to drag you back into their long-suffering sick twisted game. They are aiming to reverse the course of direction and pull you back into the harmful dangerous cycles of abuse. The reasons they do this is out of starvation from other sources of Narcissistic supply. They are low on energy and once again due to the recurring feelings of boredom and emptiness, which they are now experiencing with their present supply, they need to look elsewhere to gain new resources. You were once a good stable steady reservoir, so why not see if you're still available to feed them. There is no better way than to open old wounds from previous discarded supply and inject some fresh drama and attention, which was stopped after either you or the Narcissist carried out no contact. Coming back reignites their feelings of superiority, power and control over you as your usefulness was just being shelved, lying dormant ready for when the Narcissist saw fit to crawl back out from underneath their rock. I can assure you the only reason they are back is for their own gain and gratification.

The sole purpose of it is for the Narcissist to get what they want. They want something off you as they are now either bored with the present supply, running out of supply, lonely and need desperately some attention, sex, validation, acknowledgement, money or even just for fun entertainment purposes to see how you'll react by rocking the boat and getting to push your buttons and boundaries once again. Any reason is possible – as long as it benefits the entitled Narcissist. It's not about you, it never was, never has been and never will. The Narcissists agenda is self-serving and they are only ever thinking selfishly about their own needs and wants. Nothing has changed, they are the same miserable twisted empty beings as before.

As I mentioned in an earlier chapter about the Narcissist also being co-dependent, they are always on the prowl for constant attention as they are addicted to this pattern and cannot psychologically survive without these continuous self-serving dynamics. This is why most will never completely eradicate old supply. One way or another they will keep you on the back burner- all ex lovers, friends and acquaintances. You will be classed as future supply if needed, waiting unknowingly on the reserve bench. A substitute to be contacted even after a short or long absence. They will selfishly and pretentiously try to swoop back into your life like nothing has ever happened. They may try to even take up where they left off, it's no concern to them as you are just a resource, a prop waiting to be picked back up and reused and abused for further exploitation. You need to be aware of the possibility that they could come back at any time to try and pursue you again or just to get you to at least engage with them to stir up the swarming wasps nest.

A sudden text such as *"thinking of you"*, or *"I miss you"* are sent to tug at your heartstrings. If you have previously blocked them, they can even go as far as using a different number to try to get hold of you. If that fails then they may use an old mutual friend or acquaintance to pass on a message from them. Remember they have no shame or remorse. They will use anyone to get what they want. Other surprise communication from them could be receiving a random Hoover acting as if nothing had happened and leaving an ambiguous message, just subtle enough to send out their feelers and see if you will take the bait, saying something like – *"Hey how are you"*, *"Hope you're well"*, *"What have you been up to"*, or *"You left your gym bag round mine"* – just enough to test the waters and see if you want to once again play their cruel never ending game of cat and mouse.

Some can even go as low as pretending to have a medical illness themselves or even a family member to capture your attention and get you to re- engage. *"I have been diagnosed with cancer, I really need you right now"* or *"my mum's gone into hospital"*, *"my sisters just had a car crash and I know how close you two were"*.

It doesn't matter how outrageous the lie is, they will do and use anything to hook you back into the cycle. Some may wait for a special occasion before making contact such as flowers arriving on your doorstep on Valentine's Day or an email with the words *'Happy Birthday'* appearing in your inbox. They know that you will be most susceptible on these days as they would emotionally at one time of meant something to you.

Threats of self-harm or suicide can also be applied. Narcissists will go to any length. *"If you don't reply I will do something stupid"*, *"I mean it I will hurt myself and it will be all your fault"*, *"I can't take it anymore I'm going to kill myself"*.

In a Narcissists warped world – anything goes. They have their own rule book and remember they already know your weaknesses, vulnerabilities and strengths and will play on them to their maximum benefit. Using your emotions against you by evoking jealousy, guilt, pity, joy or your compassion. They are masters of manipulation and know what buttons to push.

Texting you a pretend caring message aimed at your children *"I really miss playing football with Joe"*, *"Tell Rachel I'm sorry I won't be at her school play*, *"I saw my nephew at the weekend and it made me think about Jack"*.

Even receiving accidental messages disguised as being meant for someone else to ignite your jealousy emotion. *"I'm stuck in traffic hun, I'll be home soon"*, *"I missed you at work today"*, *"All day I couldn't stop thinking about you- you're the best girlfriend ever xxx"*.

These deliberate miscommunications are meant to dig the knife in. Just to clarify what you are missing out on and have lost. Inside you might be thinking whether you made the right decision doubting yourself ending things or if they did, then you may be deeply upset inflicting unnecessary hurt and pain on yourself by imagining him treating the new supply better than you, maybe in fact it was all your fault after all – you were the problem as he seems so happy with the new one.

'**PING**' you receive a new friend request on social media, your heart starts to quicken as you realise it's a message from your ex Narcissist. Or even contact, which suggests you got in touch with them first *" Sorry I missed your call?"*, *"Did you just ring/text me?"*

This is another reverse tactic to get you to engage and ignite a response from you even if it's just for you to reply stating the obvious you don't know what they're talking about, you haven't called them etc. Whatever words you reply with, it worked as you fell straight into their trap of them getting a response from you and now they can ignore you and disappear once again to give you a mindf**k and leave you in a tailspin or to carry on the communication to manipulate you further.

What ever manoeuvre tactic they use, be under no illusion it is not for a genuine reconciliation and they've realised the error of their ways.

Maybe even a possible show of turning up at your house declaring their undying love for you whilst expressing fake apologies - *"You are my soulmate"*, *"You are the only one I have ever loved, please give me another chance"*, *"I'm sorry for the way I treated you, we are meant to be together"*, Or *"Please forgive me, I promise I have changed and it won't happen again"*.

These regretful pretend acknowledgements and declarations are designed to be over the top and what you have secretly been waiting, wanting to hear. There magnetic pull resonates with your inner hopes and desires and you may feel a deep relief after thinking to yourself 'yes this is exactly what I've been wanting to hear, being apart from them has made them realise how much they missed and loved me. Things will be different this time, they came back fighting for me, it's music to my ears. It's all I've ever wanted, now we can ride off into the sunset together and live happily ever after'.........

Unfortunately, victims of Narcissistic abuse can tell you a different ending – as once you go back and you think everything's rosie again you will eventually be disappointed and even retraumatized.
For the Narcissist is being on their best behaviour, they are slowly sucking you back into their twisted game, this time a watered-down version of the intense initial love bombing in the beginning. They will once again pursue you, serenade you as if you are a rare butterfly, then once you are ensnared and caught back in their net you suddenly lose your charm, unique appeal and become just another specimen who now bores and grates on the Narcissist. They will slip back into their old ways and you will find out that NOTHING HAS CHANGED.

The promises, self declarations and pledges start to crumble and you realise it was nothing more than another lie. The pathological grip may feel even tighter the next time round as they now feel invincible. By going back, the Narcissist feels even more god like and superior. In their sick minds they think how stupid you are to fall for another one of their tricks and manipulations. They now look at you even more coldly and disdainful as you obviously have no self-respect to have easily fallen and gone back to them after all the horrendous acts they have put you through.

In their eyes you are even more undeserving, worthless, needy, undesirable, dumb and pathetic. You deserve to be punished, devalued and treated badly, for you came back willingly ready for the Narcissist to psychologically wipe their dirty boots all over you again and kick you in the teeth some more.

Many victims once going back, see the cycle of abuse start to escalate and realise that there situation is even worse than the first time round. They have also had a hit to their self-esteem and confidence feeling duped and silly for believing in the Narcissists fake lies that they had changed; when in reality it couldn't be further from the truth. They may of had friends and family warn them not to go back and instead ignored their pleas and now feel embarrassed, ashamed and humiliated for not listening. These feelings in turn can make the victim feel even more stuck and trapped as they have nowhere else to turn to.

Trusting and believing in the Narcissist wanting so badly for things to work out, some go back into denial mode and stay putting up with cycles of even more bad behaviour as they feel frozen and damaged now as if they will be chastised and rebuked if they leave. Self-criticising thoughts, maybe trying to prove outsiders wrong or even thinking they are so contaminated, blemished and damaged now that no one else will want them.

Once in the throes of these addictive patterns it is even harder to break free. The predictable, repetitive cycles of **Idealise, Devalue, Discard, Hoover, Re-idealise** and so on, round and round will continue unless you drop the ball and refuse to play any more, jump off the merry go round and walk away for good. Slamming the door, locking it firmly shut, throwing away the key and sticking to no contact. Now for some going back can also have another effect, it may make them realise and actually awaken something within, which gives them the power and is a catalyst for initiating and sticking to no contact. By being treated so badly once again and being pushed so far by the Narcissist, it is the straw that broke the camel's back. Something clicks in the victim and the fuel inside bubbles up where they know there is no going back!

Once they decide to leave for good they see their true value and worth and decide they can't and will not carry on in the same s\*\*t situation with the same devastating results. They owe it to themselves to start making a stand, protecting themselves and to disengage from the Narcissist and concentrate on healing and their own lives. Remember there is a lesson behind the pain. I believe if you went back once, twice, 10 times it was because you missed something that you hadn't found in yourself and healed yet. Each time you go back you are not only learning more about how the Narcissist operates, but most importantly more about yourself.

What you will or will not tolerate, discovering limits and boundaries, any fears or insecurities you needed to face and any unhealed wounds that you had buried. It is a chance to heal, evolve and move forward in growth.

A chance to finally become stronger, wiser more attuned with your inner essence. These hard lessons are to align your inner roots and bring you back to your grounded, balanced, organic and authentic self and bring you back to the true YOU.

# Chapter 25

# High Conflict: Divorcing a Narcissist-

Ok, so by now you have realised how difficult it is cutting ties and moving on with your life if you have broken up with a Narcissist. Just count yourself one of the lucky ones if you never got married or had children with your abuser. You're still grazed and shaken from either ending the relationship or by being brutally discarded. Then on top of this you may have endured the heartache and destruction of *triangulation, smear campaign* and *hoovering*.

Well, I'm afraid that you haven't seen anything yet because things are about to get more nasty, more twisted and more dysfunctional. You will need your wits about you, as you discover finding hidden strength within, you never knew you had. It is a final test to your character, sanity and salvation. You will not have time for anymore tears as you get ready for one of the biggest battles of your life. If you think you've seen and experienced all the Narcissist's tricks and malicious schemes, you will discover it is about to become catastrophic!

As they have no further use for you anymore, their sole purpose is to bring you down to total devastation and destruction. They switch into tunnel vision mode focusing on you like a predator tearing down its prey. The Narcissists quest for your total oblivion is similar to how lions hunt for prey. Most attacks are surprisingly well organised, patient and cunning. As we know they are obsessive attention seekers and what better way to gain more than by dragging you to court. It is just another platform, a stage for them to carry on playing out their deluded fantasies. In their warped minds the courtroom is the stage, the judge is an extra (beneath them) and they are the director, producer and of course the main actor and '*you*' are the enemy!

Most 'normal' healthy people do not enjoy the thought of going into an intimidating process at an official setting in a High Court. This would no doubt be the furthest thing on their minds, trying to avoid this scenario at all costs. The stress and pain acted out in front of strangers who have the power to make decisions about your present and future would leave a bad taste in anyone's mouth. Not to mention the financial implications, the bitter atmosphere affecting children and family members. Sleepless nights of having no control over a scary uncertain situation, participating in a devastating conflict with the one person you thought you were going to spend the rest your life with. I'm sure most would choose to at least try to divorce amicably as possible for all concerned. Either by communicating and working things out in a mature manner together, between you both or if necessary using mediation as a safe, fair and calm option. This brings in someone who is impartial and neutral who doesn't take sides. It is also a lot c[...] an involving solicitors, barristers and going to cour[...]ng through a divorce is a difficult time for all involved as in most cases it is the dissolving of what was once a loving and caring partnership. Going to a family court for a resolution would be the last resort for most people. Unfortunately, when dealing with pathological dysfunctional individuals with a personality disorder it is the first and only route they are willing to go down. As they do not compromise and have no concern for you or the dissolving of the marriage, their main aim now is to 'win' at all costs.

Their ruthless selfish agenda is priority and paramount. Nothing else matters to them. They thrive off this new scenario as it gives them another opportunity to be competitive and gain more power and control. Even more so if they were the main breadwinner and know you do not have the income or resources to pay for your defence lawyers. Once again using this to their advantage to make you feel weak, insignificant and worthless. They will use the fact that if they have more money it will be another power move to continue to psychologically break you down into submission and agreement. They feed off watching you panic trying to keep afloat. They want to make things as difficult and painful for you as possible. From my own experience once my Narcissist had immediately moved on after replacing me with new supply – myself and children were of no concern. He Immediately stopped paying the mortgage knowing full well I could not afford to carry this debt on my own, ceased paying the bills and refused to pay child maintenance. He literally left me high and dry without a paddle.

Thank goodness I am blessed with amazing parents, who saved me from sinking and helped clear my arrears on the house, food and clothing for me and my children. Without their love and support I wouldn't be in the fortunate position I am now. On top of being deserted to pick up all of the pieces solo, he decided to put me through further torment by taking me to court. Due to having no hard evidence of domestic violence throughout the 16 years of emotional, psychological and physical abuse I could not gain any access to fund my case with free legal aid (*just one of the consequences of me staying silent*). Once again my family stepped in to pay for fighting my case in court and trying to secure the best future possible for me and my kids. Of course, it was just another opportunity to flaunt the new supply in front of me, trying to gauge a reaction and him hoping I would flip out at court by pushing my emotional buttons. Thankfully, I was a lot smarter than that and stayed as disengaged, robotic and business like as possible. I knew that if I reacted that was exactly what he wanted and I wasn't going to hand over any more power to him.

After staying in a bubble over 16 years, it was time to step out into reality, face the truth head on and accept how he treated me was not okay and I wasn't going to cover for his despicable behaviour any more. Once the truth was out, it was a relief that I didn't have to pretend to friends and family anymore. Most of all I didn't have to continue to lie to myself just to stay in a rut with an abuser who I had enabled by keeping quiet for him to carry on his self-serving, dysfunctional abusive antics. I finally had woken up and had to face what was directly in front of me, that the whole marriage was a sham and he was nothing more than illusion. I had held onto the false beliefs and promises from the beginning after buying into and investing in someone who never really existed. I fell in love with Dr Jekyll but married and lived in fear of Mr Hyde. Dr Jekyll was never really real only a cover, a smokescreen to hide the true ugly person behind the mask. He was a fictional character to lure me into a fantasy. Now that fantasy and realisation was finally crashing down all around me.

I had no other choice but to either fight and keep moving forward or go under. So, I collected as much information as I could; I went to the citizens advice bureau and found out what my rights were and whether I was entitled to any external help in the form of legal aid and support. You will need to stay focused and on the ball as the Narcissist will have many strategies in place to make the process as difficult as possible for you. They will purposely delay paperwork, communication and try to intimidate you as best they can.

From my own personal account my ex verbally threatened me, stating he wanted to smash my face in and used his fists to make me flinch demonstrating deliberate and purposeful hand gestures whenever we had contact in person. Therefore in the end I had to sease all contact for my own safety and go through what is called shuttle mediation. I also contacted the police and this was documented with them in case I had any further trouble.

If your partner ever bully's you and either threatens or intimidates you, and in turn you are anxious or scared for your safety then you can also contact **Refuge** or **Woman's aid** or **Men's advice line**, the latter, which is a charity that helps men suffering from domestic abuse.

Shuttle mediation in my case meant I had no physical contact with my Narcissist and it meant we were only in the same building but present separately in different rooms. We arrived and left at different points so our paths would never cross. Unfortunately, due to the nature of the Narcissist he was in no mood to negotiate fairly and especially enraged by losing the power of not having direct physical contact with me in the same room. Therefore, he refused to cooperate and instead demanded to take it to court.

Instead of the three parts being dealt with there and then i.e the divorce, property and children, he decided it would be much more entertaining to drag it out and make me suffer as much as possible both emotionally and financially. By them taking you to court they are still trying to reign their power over you. It's just another avenue to continue to go down to play their game, because you have stood up and refused to be violated any more.

If children are involved they will be used only as pawns to assist and aid the Narcissist. The healthy parent always has the children at the forefront of their minds, trying to accommodate and do everything for what's best in the interest of the children, but not the Narcissist, for their own children are just props to be used in battle. All they think and care about is what is in it for them, how they can come out on top. They will deliberately cause as much friction and conflict as possible in order to carry on the abuse even when the partnership has ended. They plan on having a long drawn out settlement to add to the overwhelming stress you're already going through and also to drag out and bump up the legal fees. Never underestimate what a Narcissist is capable of, as remember they have no empathy, take no accountability or responsibility for anything, feel entitled and are masters of deception and manipulation. Going to court is just another playground for them to play in.

Putting forward my side of the petition in the divorce proceedings with one of the reasons being his adultery. At first he tried his best to deny this fact but after I had evidence of him engaged and living with the new supply he finally had no choice but to admit it. After his admission, it should've been a straightforward case but of course he still wanted to gain the upper hand and to control the situation; so he would only agree to admitting and signing his adultery on two conditions. One if I didn't name the other woman as the co-respondent and secondly I had to pay fully on my own for the divorce. To me the price was worth paying just to legally dissolve the marriage and move another step closer to beginning a new life.

If I could give you some helpful advice when dealing with the children side of things (if any are involved) I would definitely recommend you gain a court order of schedule. This was a life saver for me and means it is fixed for both parties with a schedule of what's in the best interest of the children and lays out and permits anything you think is important such as days and times of contact and handovers, holidays, weekends, special occasions, whether the pick up/drop offs will be through a contact centre or any exchanges carried out by family and friends. It is one of the most important documents you will have to adhere by and will help you to keep your sanity for when the Narcissist tries to diverge from any fixed plans or arrangements. Because it is summoned through the court, and written in legal stone the Narcissist is less likely to ignore the requests and will give you peace of mind.

If they ever say otherwise, which most will try to push in the beginning as they don't like boundaries or rules and they will feel like they are losing control, always refer back to the court order and reinstate and repeat to the Narcissist the requests are set out clearly and remind them if they are unclear of anything then to refer back to their copy of the order.

I also had enforced on mine only contact via email or text messaging, which meant no phone calls so I didn't have to go through the torment of communicating and hearing his voice. Also because he was abusive he was not allowed to come within a certain distance of my house, so again I had complete peace of mind I could relax in my haven knowing full well he couldn't ever just turn up on my door step and only other allocated parties who I agreed to could come to my house for pick ups and hand overs. It meant I could heal and start to feel safe in my own home and disengage from anymore toxic exchanges with my ex Narcissist.

From a distance I was strong enough to learn to disengage and respond only to the facts.

If you are one of the unfortunate ones who has to do any handovers in person then I still suggest exactly the same responses. Stay strong, learn to be assertive and never let them get you off track by attempting to get you to engage in anything but the children. If they attempt this shut them down at the first opportunity and do not accept any nonsense or communication of them trying to divert away from the relevant situation or if they try to verbally attack you. Always set strong and clear boundaries be focused and to the point, businesslike showing no emotion and you will learn to navigate this new journey called "co-parenting".

Of course, as your co-parenting with someone dysfunctional with a personality disorder I'm afraid there is no cookie cutter way of doing things. You will need to adapt, will still be hyper vigilant and you will even find with the court order in place they will still try to rock your boat, but over time hopefully things may settle down while they refocus on a new victim and you will find relief in rediscovering your freedom. Also knowing that this nightmare isn't forever as your children will one day grow into adults themselves and as long as they have 'you', the stable, healthy loving, caring, compassionate and empathetic supportive constant role model in their lives they will go on to thrive and become well adjusted healthy individuals.

Going back and forth, separating the marital assets and child custody was another two battles I had to endure. It was a long, emotionally and financially draining process, which took up most of my life for over a year. When I reflect and look back now it all seems a blur.

I am now four years post divorce and have an amazing enriching, harmonious peaceful life for me and my children. We've grown as a family and are stronger and closer than ever. Even though going through a high conflict divorce with a toxic being can take the wind out of you and you may feel like giving up at times, remember to keep fighting for what you believe in, for the truth and for you and your children and to continue to surround yourself with loving, caring and supportive family and friends you can rely on and be your rock during this turbulent transition; as I guarantee you will need them. They are there for you, so never be afraid to reach out and ask for help. You will get through it even in your darkest moments. You will transform from victim into a warrior and will make an amazing journey and life for yourself.

*Show the Narcissist they underestimated you and only you have the power over your life.*

# Chapter 26

# Navigating the choppy waters when children are involved!

Okay, so after you have survived the traumatic divorce with your Narcissistic ex you still unfortunately have the ongoing battle of navigating contact if children are involved. No contact unfortunately in some cases is not an option as your ex may have 50% parental rights. In this scenario you are striving to go to *Low contact* as much as possible. Your main aim is to protect your child/children and buffer the toxic impact to lessen the long lasting emotional psychological destruction. You can help them to develop coping skills by listening, encouraging and validating their feelings, which will in time help them to gain confidence and resilience. Always remember the Narcissists motive, everything they do is for their own agenda to take advantage of you and to make themselves appear outwardly in a positive light.

You cannot reason or appeal to their good nature as it doesn't exist. Of course your dealing with the most precious thing in the world-your children and the Narcissist knows this full well and will use this natural parent vulnerability against you. Give them nothing to use as ammo and nothing to feed off. Just stick to facts and have unemotional exchanges.

As I briefly mentioned previously another important step would be to include any contact information regarding the children using a court order as a solid document to protect yourself and your children. This is a great tool to keep contact, information and guidelines adhered to in a powerful way. The order will lay out all relevant information including where and who the children will live with and when and how they will spend time with each parent.

It is a legally binding contract, which is similar to a parenting plan – it covers the main practical issues and helps everyone to understand what is involved and expected of them. It is also a very valuable reference to get the Narcissist to refer back to if they start playing up and try to cause different arrangements, conflict and friction. It sets out logistics, times, dates, contact arrangements and can include any education or health care of the child/ren involved. Every order will be different to the next person and will depend on circumstances, ages, needs and wishes of the children.

The contact will state whether it be for long or short periods of time and will include information on any overnight stays. The court order will be generated, most likely when you're dealing with an unreasonable, self-absorbed person such as a Narcissist. This is when both parties cannot agree to make any mutual decisions.

Therefore, the court order is a useful strategy to be put into place to help resolve any present or future disagreements which may arise. You will both negotiate and put forward your wishes, but ultimately if you cannot both reach an agreement the court will issue a child agreements order, which will impose the decision of contact arrangements which they feel are in the best interests of the children.

In my own personal circumstances, I had two children with my ex toxic partner. The court order of contact was completely different for each of my children. If there has been any abuse whether being physical or emotional and psychological then a team of welfare officers will intervene and want to speak to your child/ren for their input, wishes and needs. The conclusion was no physical contact was allowed with my eldest, my son, which he personally stated due to his Dad being mostly verbally threatening, constant anger rages but also physically crossing the barriers by clipping him round the head if he saw red or by shouting, screaming and spitting in his face while having one of his many volcanic eruptions. With a constant involvement of him starting arguments for no reason with either my son or myself, just to cause some kind of commotion, drama or abusive conflict.

As I mentioned earlier, if your ex has a full blown personality disorder then trying to appeal to them and get a normal humane response is futile. A scary first hand example of this was when my son fell severely ill one night and was potentially life threatening. A gradual rash of weals appeared over his body while his eyes started to swell up and clamp shut leaving him unable to open them and gradually to the point of having difficulty breathing and his lips turning blue- for he was having an anaphylactic reaction. I started screaming at my ex to help and do something to which I'll never forget his eerie heartless response while staring into his cold reptile soulless eyes as he calmly said "I'm going to bed now, goodnight", turned and walked away leaving me in a state of shock. I soon snapped out of it and put my son in the car and drove him to the nearest A&E (accident and emergency) department where they gave him the adrenaline he needed to fight the trigger and recover overnight in hospital.

After that my son had to carry an epi-pen on him and thank goodness he's had no serious episodes since. But you can imagine how gut wrenching it was for my son to witness how callous and cruel his own father could be. Of course disturbing accounts of his unloved childhood and trauma were reflected and respected in the court and the outcome was his father only being allowed to send him a letter once a month. This safety net was a chance for my son to grow to begin to feel safe and express himself. His father sent maybe three letters in the whole 4 years since no contact and each one was predictably written informing him about himself and his wonderful Narcissistic perfect life. My son is thriving since cease of contact and is so much happier, safe and secure now he doesn't have to tiptoe on egg shells anymore.

My daughter on the other hand due to her fathers anger and rages being less directed at her, unfortunately in the courts eyes the father is still allowed access. Their justifications are just because he has been abusive to the Mother and one child doesn't necessarily mean he will do the same to the other child. Therefore, they would rather give him a chance to prove that he can step up and start playing a proper father figure. As I'm sure you can imagine from my own personal experience it was traumatising to say least. I felt like I couldn't protect my little girl and I was sending her off like a lamb into the lion's den. The only way the courts will keep her safe and cease no contact would be if he put a foot wrong. But it is emotionally and mentally painful waiting, knowing that any moment behind close doors her father could blow up and suddenly switch from Mr nice fake daddy into an overpowering monster. Even though my daughter had grown up in a toxic environment with her Dad, witnessing him attacking me and her brother she was far too young and vulnerable to be capable to make the decision not to see him, she was only six at the time of our divorce. I'm lucky that him having other women (new victims) to focus on will one redirect his anger and vengeance but also is an extra shield for my daughter as he will be trying to impress them by portraying his sweet best daddy of the year act. On top of this limited contact of only every other weekend and a couple of hours after school one day a week enforces her protection. I would recommend using a communication book to take with them if younger children are involved and as they get older giving them a mobile phone to stay in touch if they are worried or anxious going around to the other parents house, it will give you and them peace of mind if they need to get hold of you.

In my own circumstances, all physical exchanges are carried out through an agreed third party. Either friends or family. Someone you trust and is impartial for the handovers. So it's been four years now that myself and my son have had no physical contact and four years of my daughter having limited contact. It's not always easy to navigate and I still have to respect the choice of her seeing her biological father. The minute I hear his mask has slipped and she is in any kind of danger that will be his last chance. I will always be there to love and protect her the best I can, in the circumstances I've been faced with. She will be old enough one day to make up her own mind. She's seen and heard enough as a child and I do not need to influence her in anyway. I will always try to be honest and open with my children and support them in any way I can. One day her father will show his true colours all by himself, and if her world of fake daddy crumbles, then I will be there to pick up the pieces and comfort her as best I can. I will continue to teach her right from wrong, to be kind, respectful and authentic. As she gets older I will educate her on healthy relationships, what is acceptable and what is not. She will be well influenced to make healthy choices in life and never put up with any domestic violence within a relationship. I know she is a bright, intelligent young lady who will grow up to be a well adjusted, balanced healthy and capable adult. This process and set up isn't ideal, but then I never did sign up to be married or have children with a manipulative abuser. I've had to learn and adapt to new challenging circumstances, which have been thrown at me and will continue to do so as I face further adversity along the way.

If your children's arrangements never reach court then you can always create your own parenting plan and possibly try and get it legally binding by a solicitor. I would also suggest, in any scenario when dealing with the Narcissist or a toxic person to document absolutely everything. Otherwise it's always a battle of He said/ She said. Always save any communication and correspondence by email or messages and if you ever receive any abusive texts you can always screenshot them for evidence. Another useful tool for the exchange of communication would be to use third-party apps such as *our family wizard*. It's a mobile responsive service, which provides a secure location to document, store and share information about your custodial or parenting plan. I would definitely recommend to use a site such as this to help eliminate extra stress, worry, miscommunication and to avoid any unnecessary arguments, which we all know Narcissists love to create and thrive off. It's a useful tool to include all of the ongoing difficult situations, which may arise such as children's schooling, medical needs, birthdays, Christmases and any special occasions etc.

Holiday schedules and calendars on the app give you the opportunity to update each other on any unexpected changes or new agreements. Either by using the dedicated site exchanging contact information or via personal email or text messaging, the main theme is to be in control, state any facts and never stray from the subject at hand. This includes any personal handovers as even the simplest exchange can still be turned into a hostile conflict of events unless you quickly learn to disengage, set firm and clear boundaries, stick to facts to discuss only information regarding anything to do with the children and one of the most important key tools is to show no emotion!

I personally would also recommend separating important dates as much as possible. By arranging and attending separate birthdays, family parties, Christmases and any schooling scenarios such as sports days or parents evenings. To a Narcissist these will be just another opportunity to attack you and further push your emotional buttons and get you to engage. Co-parenting with a Narcissist is not an easy process at any stage of your child's development but the sooner you learn to detach, exchange business like only communication, the sooner the Narcissist will realise you are refusing to play any more of their twisted games and they are solo, unable to use you as an energy source any more.

# Chapter 27

# Dating again in the future-

I know in this moment in time the word dating again probably horrifies you and is the last thing on your mind. But depending where you are on your journey, here are some helpful tips and suggestions to support you if and when you are ready to dip your toes back into the dating scene.

To help yourself, in the future to aid stopping from gravitating towards the same kind of dysfunctional toxic relationships, you will need to make yourself aware of the red flags and be conscious of who you get close to and let into your life. This should only be done though once you have healed and have spent enough time on your own, rebuilding your self-esteem and confidence. After you have picked up all of the pieces and are finally happy, content and feeling in a good peaceful place. It would be destructive and counter-productive to get into another relationship quickly before you have healed your wounds from the trauma you have experienced.
Never try and take a shortcut or try and get a quick fix to fill the empty, lonely void you may be feeling. You need to get to the bottom of why you have an attraction to Narcissists/Toxic people and relationships and figure out

and heal the parts of yourself that are vulnerable to these emotional and controlling vampires.

You will then be fully equipped to go on in, eyes wide open, your spidery feelers working and having the confidence to listen to your gut/intuition early on and mostly be able to trust yourself.

Hopefully, you would of learned how to be more assertive and how to create and stick to healthy boundaries, choosing ones which are right for "*you*".

Owning your own agency enforcing your own boundaries and believing in yourself so that you do deserve to be treated kindly, lovingly and with total respect.

If anyone tries to push or break your boundaries then you know they are not right for you and to quickly exit and walk away. Do not waste your time or invest in people who bring you harm. We all get lonely at different points in our lives but it's understanding that this doesn't have to be a bad thing and can actually be a great opportunity to focus on the things you love to do and concentrate on yourself and your needs. It's a chance and time to reconnect with your inner self.

Especially after being in a toxic relationship it is important to spend the no-contact time getting to rediscover and know yourself inside and out. There is no magic wand, it takes time and effort but the results are worth it as you will be more likely to attract healthy, worthy individuals in the future. Stay strong and centred and if you do find yourself dating again, remember to carry on doing the things you love and never give up on your hobbies, friends, interests, tastes and dreams to please a new person. Always remember you are enough just as you are and the right person will love and respect you for that and encourage and support you to be the best version of yourself. The right person will not bring you down and belittle you. They will not play mind games and devalue you. You will be an equal team, supporting one another with genuine kind intentions who will have each other's back and best interests at heart.

You will know when you find it, and you will feel so relaxed, happy and secure together it will never be a one-sided toxic game that you had with the Narcissist. Never again walking on eggshells, you will know exactly where you stand and the relationship will be transparent, sincere and flow positively, just an easy feeling where you don't have to try so hard. Just a natural and organic union. You will both be able to communicate in a safe, caring environment and be able to listen to what the other person is saying in an understanding and supportive way and both be heard. You will reassure each other, nurture and grow the relationship into a deep meaningful partnership. Resolving any issues or problems, which is inevitable even in the best relationships and to do so in an adult caring and patient manner. If you are feeling lonely wanting desperately to be loved, or feel like you need someone else until you can be happy and complete then you are definitely not ready to start dating again. You have to learn to be happy, content and fulfilled on your own authenticity - only then can you start entertaining the idea of getting involved in a romantic relationship.

We need to get to a place where we accept ourselves. Realising that we are worthy of genuine love, emotional support and respect. You may have undealt wounds from childhood that need addressing or self-esteem issues. It's important to self-reflect and go on a journey within to find out what parts are missing or need healing. We need to practice self-compassion, self-respect and acceptance so we are careful who we let into our lives and repel any dysfunctional individuals who display any unacceptable behaviours and actions.

We do have a **choice** and we do have a **voice**, it is up to us to act on it and start empowering ourselves to use it.

Remember some well-known sayings *"we only continue to put up with what we allow", "teach people how you want to be treated" and "believe people the first time that they show you who they are".*

This positive mindset will help you to show others what your standards are and what you will or will not tolerate. If anyone crosses or pushes your boundaries then these are not people you want or need in your life. You must learn to change the way you treat yourself and in turn show and tell others what you deserve and what is acceptable or not acceptable.

If you don't and you carry on in denial, in silence then you will continue the same patterns and go into more dysfunctional relationships.

This saying by Tony Gaskins rings true- *"you teach people how to treat you, by what you allow, what you stop, and what you reinforce".*

Please start by raising the bar and truly loving and accepting yourself even all your flaws that you don't like. Embrace yourself, every part of you. It's important to understand by loving yourself you are NOT being 'selfish' or turning into a Narcissist. You are still your caring, compassionate self but now someone who respects and loves themselves so much that you will never again allow another abuser to insult or disrespect you in anyway. You will immediately put a stop to it and speak up. For you now value yourself and know your worth.

**Below are some acclaimed inspirational quotes-**

*"Stop asking why they keep doing it and start asking, why you keep allowing it"*

*"People think being alone makes you lonely, but I don't think that's true. Being surrounded by the wrong people is the loneliest thing in the world"*

*"People only treat you one way.....
the way you allow them"*

*"Throughout life people make you mad, disrespect you and treat you bad. Let God deal with the things they do, cause hate in your heart will consume you too"*

*"What you allow, is what will continue"*

*"No one can hurt you without your permission"*

*"Some people can be mean and treat you poorly. Don't take it personally. It says nothing about you, but everything about them"*

*"If you aren't being treated with <u>love</u> and <u>respect</u>, check your price tag. Maybe you've marked yourself down. It's you who tells people <u>what you're worth</u>. Get off the clearance rack and get behind the glass where they keep the <u>valuables</u>"*

# Chapter 28

# WHY Healthy Individuals get into relationships?

1.  Healthy individuals want to get into a relationship because they are already happy in themselves and want to share their love and happiness with another individual. Healthy people value their time and their love and therefore want to invest/share this special gift, caring about another person and creating a deep connection with joy of building a future together.

2.  It is a wonderful feeling to know that your partner is always there to support you and vice versa. Knowing you can rely on each other no matter what, through the good times and the bad. Understanding one another's strengths and weaknesses and picking one another up if the others feeling low. Being a rock, looking out and wanting the best for each other. Maybe after a bad day at work listening, supporting or trying to cheer the other up, whilst having empathy and compassion to build a solid and long lasting healthy relationship.

3.  Even though it is important to enjoy and value your alone time and great to keep your own independence, individual hobbies and friends, it is also nice to share these things together at times and enjoy each other's company and have fun and explore new and exciting adventures together. You learn to grow together and create happy memories and you get to bounce your ideas, hopes and dreams and open up to new suggestions, experiences, challenges and tastes etc and share these together in an exciting mutual way.

4.  To have a close bond with someone to maybe experience the joys of marriage and having children, in a loving and caring mutual relationship.

5.  To learn and grow with genuine intentions, deeply caring about each other even if you are are upset with something the other person has done, you still think about their feelings and not wanting to cause any unnecessary pain. You both should feel safe expressing your feelings, needs and desires without it threatening the relationship. Being honest and upfront with another where you can talk openly about anything builds a close bond that reaffirms your commitment. That includes being able to both apologise when in the wrong and take accountability and responsibility for your part if and when it arises and trust the fact that by

owning up to any mistakes and apologizing that your significant other will still love you.

6. You are both wanting to be honest in your motives and offer stability, reliability, security and are dependable being able to rely on each other and know if either of you says you'll do something, then you know you can trust them on their word and they will follow through with actions. They are consistent on their promises and deliver with no hidden agenda.

7. We are social creatures and want to connect and create a secure bond with another human being and share our unique journey together. You may decide you get on so well and compliment each other bringing a greater richness to each other's lives. Healthy relationships can contribute to dealing with stress easier when feeling supported and also statistically shown living longer when in strong, solid partnerships.

8. To find love and give love. Love should be about bringing out the best in each other. In a healthy relationship you can both compromise and act less selfishly. You want to share and help the other making you both better people in the process, naturally demonstrating your love, flexibility and caring compassionate nature to improve and work together as a team. Aiming towards a mutual goal of building a solid, thriving foundation of love and trust to continue a future union of growth.

# Chapter 29

# WHY Narcissists get into Relationships?

1. Narcissists do 'NOT' get into relationships for the same reasons that healthy individuals do. It is a move that is pure survival to them. Without constant supply the Narcissist feels dead inside. They are always on the hunt for new prey whether already in one relationship, or will have others at the ready behind the scenes to fall into when leaving one. At times some will even overlap. It makes no difference to the Narcissist as long as they have someone to use to avoid the forever nagging void inside of them.

2. The Narcissists whole reason is self-serving to 'USE' another person. Whether that be for company, sex, money, food, a home, status whatever they see fit, it depends upon what you have to offer them.

3. Due to them never wanting to be alone, they will do everything to avoid this. They need people for attention, admiration and validation to make them feel like they exist. Your attention gives them energy and they continually suck it out of you like a vampire. After they get bored of the initial 'fake

romance' of receiving positive fuel, they start the devaluation stage to spice things up a bit and also as now they are confident you are hooked they start to get comfortable, so they let their mask slip.

So, even now when they are getting a negative fuel out of you it still satisfies and fulfills them in exactly the same way – good or bad fuel is the same thing as (attention/energy). It makes no difference to a Narcissist, either way you are feeding them and they are getting their fix, which confirms that they have an affect on you and they are important and it makes them feel alive.

4.  Some also get into relationships as you make them look good. You are being used as it makes them appear more normal to the outside world and supports their delusional fantasies of ideal love. They want to seem to come across as normal as possible even though they are far from it. You help them by being a prop to cover up their true intentions.

5.  Another reason is Narcissists are very jealous and envious beings. In their warped minds if they see you have something of value to them they think just by being with you, by association it will rub off on the Narcissist and they will gain some of your value that they want. In the beginning you are a new shiny toy to be played with.

6. Deep down Narcissists feel so out of control and crave power and to control their significant other as it makes them feel back in the driving seat. They are always constantly battling to get the upper hand and dominate the relationship, in order to make their false world seem safer and more secure.

7. Due to their fake persona they fear being alone so they are always on the prowl for new objects (aka people) to give them an ego boost.

8. Directly because of the Narcissists own insecurities and flaws, they get into a relationship to distract themselves from these things and to project them onto his/her partners. You are there to serve them and be their emotional punching bag and even sometimes used as a physical one.

9. A high percentage of Narcissists overlap to the disorder of sociopathy and therefore can be sadists. They get into relationships as they enjoy being manipulative, playing games and hurting others. They get a kick out of it. As they have no empathy or remorse it is an enjoyable sport to them.

10. They need others as a mirror to reflect back to them their false-self as they can't bear to be alone with their own thoughts and deep seated wounds. The fake mask they have created in their mind is constructed as being perfect so getting this reassurance and feedback is crucial to the Narcissist.

11. Also so they can continue to use and triangulate their    victims with their next supply even after being discarded.

# Chapter 30

# Personal Boundaries-

True love and respect cannot exist without boundaries. You need to change any old negative belief patterns, which don't serve you and are not in your best interest anymore. Create new loving self-compassionate and self-caring beliefs, which are designed to protect you and support your overall well-being. Setting boundaries and seeing them through isn't being selfish either – it's self-love. By learning to face your fears and inner demons, only then can you begin to realise you don't need another's love or approval, you have the power to give yourself those things and only then when you truly appreciate loving and cherishing yourself will you be able to be healthy enough to feel maybe you would like to share your pure love with another.

We can't give our love unless we are filled with love. When you are ready to learn, grow and openly love, it should hopefully be a mutual union of both being self-fulfilled and having a capacity to share these unique qualities and companionship on a deeper level. So once you have spent the time needed to reflect and heal any inner wounds, you will be better equipped going forward.

I would also suggest it is a good idea to identify and set certain personal boundaries, which will guide and help protect you in any future dating ventures. At first it may seem foreign and difficult, but the more you practice and enforce healthy boundaries into your life, the more you will be grateful for doing so. You need to get in touch with your inner self and gain knowledge and a better understanding of who you are, your feelings, your thoughts, your wants, needs and things you desire, things that make you happy and content. Stick to your values, morals and any old or new beliefs which serve you. Act on these from the beginning and if anyone crosses your personal boundaries let them know it will not be tolerated.

If your partner infringes on your boundaries and you let them do so more than once, you are inviting them to repeat these actions over and over again. It's important about being open, honest and transparent so both parties know each other's limits. Communication, compromise and respect will be needed and you should both feel free to express your wants and needs in a mutual loving relationship. If your partner gets angry or deliberately crosses a boundary you have set, then that is your alarm to listen up and take note that they are not showing you the respect and courtesy you deserve.

You may have a list of non-negotiable healthy boundaries, which once crossed will end in you saying adios to the relationship. A few examples of these could be if your partner cheats on you either by kissing, sexual contact or intercourse, you set your own limits and what you will or will not put up with. You might show them the door if they verbally/emotionally or physically hurt you, or if they lie constantly and disrespect you. If they are controlling and selfish or one-sided everything has to be on their terms. Maybe if they are flaky and playing childlike push/pull games, or being inconsistant and unreliable saying one thing but doing another. Maybe you will show them the door if they are using recreational drugs or drinking excessively. Other reasons could be if they are showing no compassion or empathy.

They are set by you and each person's will be different to another's. If your boundaries are ever crossed and violated- always take action. Boundaries are your powerful and healthy layer of protective armour. They help you to get what you want, need and expect from a relationship and also help you spot signs early on if something or someone isn't quite right for you. Having a clear idea will save you time and heartache further down the road. It stops toxic people walking all over you and pushing you to do things that make you uncomfortable. Without any healthy boundaries you have people take advantage of you and you leave yourself open to disrespect and abuse. You may of found it hard to say 'NO' in the past to even the simplest of things, as you may of been a natural co-dependent and a people pleaser.

It is necessary, worthwhile and rewarding to practice and do the work on yourself implementing healthy boundaries to be truly happy, respected and full filled from an intimate relationship.

It is important to identify what your personal boundaries are and then be willing to implement them when necessary. They can be physical, emotional, mental and verbal limits that we establish to shield ourselves from being used, manipulated or impinged upon. It is a powerful message that communicates to us that we have positive self-respect, worth and will not allow others to push our integrity.

It is your right and responsibility to show others how to treat you. When establishing clearly defined guidelines I think it is also important to trust your instincts and any gut feelings to help assist with your personal values. You have to be your own advocate and know yourself well.

1. Start by doing the inner work to heal any old wounds, any past bad experiences and negative programmings.
2. Tap in deep to yourself in order to recognise and identify your own feelings.
3. Take the time to acknowledge and understand what you want or don't want in a relationship; what you will or will not tolerate.
4. Identify what standards you expect and what consequences will be implemented if they are crossed.
5. A healthy relationship is also about balance, so in turn make sure you are respecting your partner's personal boundaries.
6. Having mutual boundaries you are supporting one another and building a foundation of trust and respect.

As you grow together your boundaries may change at certain points in your relationship. As long as you both communicate any changes with open honesty, you can be sure your both on the same page and can once again strengthen your partnership.

# Chapter 31

# Transformation-

*Feelings when the toxic relationship ends-*

You will be sinking in stress hormones and likely to become withdrawn and depressed. Love is just as addictive as drugs and when you are cut off from your long term drug aka the Narcissist, your body and mind will go through withdrawals. It is very common to experience depression and anxiety after a traumatic experience such as this. Even though you were exposed to these low feelings during the abusive relationship, your self-esteem and self-confidence will plummet even further. When in the midst of it as I know myself, even though the abuser may have been physically present they were emotionally absent, which meant the majority of the time I felt alone and single anyway. Anxiety levels will hit the roof the same way a drug addict feels anxious when they need a fix and the only way to relieve the anxiety is to re-connect with our love addiction object.

On top of that, experiencing overwhelming ruminating thoughts which hijack your emotions can leave you unable to carry out even the simplest of tasks. After abuse we have selective memory where the addictive brain torches us by continually thinking about only the 'good times' in the relationship, burying and turning a blind eye to the bad. You may of been so dependent on your abuser that you now feel completely lost and broken without them. Yearning for their toxic presence to return even after all the abuse you've endured is a normal feeling. You had been so brainwashed and downtrodden, while existing in the relationship that you overwhelmingly feel like you won't be able to survive without them. Standing alone to begin to pick up all of the broken pieces and start finding you again, feels foreign to you. You need to rebuild an identity which was stolen. A new purpose to focus on and create a new chapter, one without abuse, suffering and codependency. A chance to rediscover your buried 'self' and reawaken what was taken away from you.

# Healing and Recovery-

Undoing the damage caused by "cognitive dissonance" is an individual process where the survivor needs to begin to receive validation and confirmation by going over parts of the abuse and trauma by replaying the narrative either verbally or by journaling their personal experiences. This reduces the anxiety and is replaced in time by balance and equilibrium and once again by being grounded in reality. Not the fake reality the Narcissist manufactured.

It's about having your voice finally heard, identifying events for what they were and consciously facing up to the truth of what you really experienced.

Recovering from this type of continued histrionic abuse can leave survivors suffering from Post Traumatic Stress Disorder (PTSD). It can be scary for the individual experiencing it as even though the actual traumatic event maybe over, in real time it still feels like a continuous nightmare as the events keep playing out in the survivors mind, over and over replaying disturbing personal experiences they were subjected to. It is reliving the past in the present moment either by having flashbacks, nightmares or reoccurring unwanted images or sensations. Symptoms can be mentally tormenting or can take on physical form such as sweating, palpitations, trembling and overwhelming feelings of loss of control with heightened anxiety and hypervigilance. Difficulty concentrating and sleep problems such as insomnia are also common.

One useful method of treatment for PTSD is Eye Movement Desensitisation and Reprocessing (EMDR).
Another therapy is (CBT) which is a trauma focused Cognitive Behavioural Therapy which helps individuals talk about and face up to the traumatic event/s, so that they learn to cope and challenge any distress or unwanted negative thought patterns consuming them. By identifying and ultimately gaining control of the fear, accepting what happened and consciously understanding it cannot hurt you anymore. Thoughts are not you, your experiences are not you. You can retrain your brain to manage your symptoms and this begins by opening up, talking and gaining insight into your past of emotional anguish.

# *Managing withdrawal symptoms-*

Best course of action and the most important first step you will need to take, is by going cold turkey, detaching and having **NO CONTACT** whatsoever with your abuser. This gives time for the mind and body to heal, detoxify and stabilise in a safe, calm and predictable secure retreat. You need close friends, parents, family and maybe even outside help to support you including other sources such as counsellors, therapists etc.

You may also need to see a doctor for medication to ease any ongoing anxiety and depression after coming to terms with the trauma you faced. You need to learn and undo all of the false beliefs the Narcissist brainwashed you into believing.

You are strong, you are worthy and you are enough – more than enough. You always have been. You need to learn that you cannot control your partners behaviour, you are not to blame, you cannot fix or save them, no matter how desperately you want to or believe that it's necessary for you to do so. It is the abuser's responsibility, their problem and are solely accountable for their shady actions. Your decision making skills are likely to be poor as for so long you have not trusted yourself and relied instead on the words and actions of the Narcissist. You will need to learn to trust your judgement, gut instinct and intuition. As well as normal everyday things such as re discovering and exploring your own likes/dislikes, tastes, music, hobbies, choices and desires that have been eroded, and taken over all these months or years. Treatment to help in this area is practice and patience to empower individuals to develop, strengthen and start to trust their own decision-making abilities.

Neuroplasticity makes it possible for our brains to make new neural connections and pathways in positive and productive ways. Such as exercise, healthy eating, wellbeing, new interests and mixing with other healthy people socially. Train yourself and start self-practice by giving yourself healthier rewards and obsessions – anything that is in your best interest. Things and people who will validate, support and nurture you rather than those unhealthy bonds which starve us and leave us reeling for our next fix of crumbs. Join online forums, support groups and classes where other survivors can express their own experiences to validate and support each other. By connecting with others who have gone through similar events will empower you to speak your truth and know you are not alone.

I know for my own journey in the beginning it helped greatly by going online and finding Narcissistic abuse forums. I could read other similar accounts which supported and validated my toxic experiences. Beforehand I had never even heard of the term 'Narcissist' and it felt as if a light switch had been turned on by sourcing and comparing how eerily similar and accurate other survior stories were compared to my own personal accounts. This was my first epiphany which opened my eyes and set me on my path to freedom!

As well as going 'No Contact' it is also a good idea to remove/avoid things that may trigger your addiction. You will need to avoid places you know he/she will be or where you both frequently visited, places when you were dating etc. At least until you feel a lot stronger down the line when you know you are finally in a good place mentally and emotionally fully detached. Another useful idea is to get rid of any memorabilia that remind you of your abuser. These can include photographs, clothes, gifts and letters. You can either throw these away as a detox or burn them and have a shift in awareness that you are disposing of all the negativity these items bring when associated with your ex Narcissist. It is a very empowering exercise as you transform into a new positive state. You can go out and replace these items with anything that makes you smile and brings you joy.

# Chapter 32

# Keep putting one foot in front of the other-

Mostly be patient with yourself and give yourself time to heal. At first, you may feel like isolating yourself in the beginning of recovery. Try to get out, little by little and start making some positive plans with other people. Start off by doing small things that you used to enjoy, things for yourself. Buy that new shampoo, dye your hair a different colour, have a nice bubble bath, read an inspiring book, watch a funny film, light a new candle and recreate a calm tranquil atmosphere for you to unwind down and feel safe in. It doesn't matter how small or how simple the gesture is, just make sure it is something that brings YOU joy and happiness.

I also found helpful getting out and about walking my dog, even though I didnt feel like doing so at the time. He gave me a purpose and a focus to get out of the house, breathe fresh air and in turn calm my mind and racing thoughts. Just cuddling him and feeling his love and warmth kept me going. Maybe you could borrow a friends pet if you dont have any of your own, as they are proven to bring down anxiety and stress levels and even just by being around them can help you to release feel good hormones.

The first few hours, days and weeks will be the hardest, but I promise you it will get easier even if it doesn't feel that way right now. Just concentrate on putting one foot in front of the other, focus on you and your healing. Be kind and compassionate to yourself. Remind yourself that this is a temporary state of mind and you will start to feel stronger and slowly regain your centre and identity.
Another thing that helped me a great deal was by marking on the calendar each day of '**No Contact**'. This empowed me to keep going as I could visually see and feel myself starting to take my power back and gain some control. As the weeks, months pass and you document this progression daily on your calendar you will begin to feel so much stronger and more capable to stick to no contact knowing it is the right decision and the **ONLY** decision; the only way to truly propel you into self recovery. Remember you are on a journey back to yourself.

Over the time you have spent – (wasted) with your Narcissist you probably don't know who you are anymore. I myself felt numb and lost, I was a shell of my former self and felt like I had lost my identity. My whole life was fixated and entwined with my abuser, I had to rediscover who I was. I was unrecognisable in the mirror having no self-esteem or confidence left. I was emotionally and mentally drained, exhausted from the continuous trauma I had experienced. To be alone for the first time in my life felt very foreign and uncertain. I had to learn to be comfortable in my own body and skin. I had no choice but to sit, experience and accept the discomfort. Feel what it's like truly being by myself and slowly learnt that I was going to be okay.

Once some time has passed and you start to feel the fog lifting, you can start to gain some clarity back. You will be able to take a step back from all the chaos and trauma you experienced and really get a grip of reality and the realisation of what you went through. At this point you may still be ruminating and having unwanted thoughts and the best way to expel these negative intrusions would be to try meditation.

This will give your mind and body a break from all the constant to-ing and fro-ing of craziness still going through your mind. By quelling and silencing the mind, you begin to relax and start to feel calm and balanced again. I find meditation is almost like a reset button, which puts the brakes on all the rambling and nuisance thoughts, which can start to build up and over ride your life once they start to take momentum. It is a big step forward to change your way of thinking, by understanding only you control your thoughts, you choose and allow what goes in and out and ultimately have the power to not let any negative thoughts and in turn emotions affect you. Meditation takes time and patience but is a useful tool in your well-being and healing process. There are many different types to try to get you to focus on the now, in the moment, the present as this is all each of us can truly experience anyway. Too many of us are stuck in the past or fixated on the future, which is not constructive. The past is gone and cannot be changed only lessons learnt, and the future hasn't come or may never come so you need to start enjoying the only existence which is upon you and that is the NOW.

You can start off by using a body scan or by listening to general peaceful relaxation music. Once you get into slowing your mind down and concentrating on your breathing then you can move onto more specific guided meditation samples.

Most of your thoughts are broken records which have been programmed and turned habitable in force. They can be repetitive negative connotations, which you may feel like you have no other choice than to keep hearing and playing the old beat of the drum. You need to become aware that you are the master of your own universe, you can play a new record, create a new story, indulge in new experiences with new ideas and outcomes.

You can start by slowing your mind down into a relaxed state and then reprogramming your brain by exposing it to positive reinforcements using frequent happy, upbeat, joyful positive self-praise and affirmations, which start the momentum rolling in the right direction. It will have a snowball effect, the more good and calm you introduce into your life the stronger and longer it will stay. They will formulate into new healthy thought patterns, which in turn, flips your emotions around to you now feeling good vibrations. Just like the old false negative junk mail in your brain was a habit, the new positive thoughts will also become habit and will change your overall outlook on life.

You will clearly be able to see what you went through wasn't your fault, you are not to blame and you realise how lucky you are to be free from the toxic drama. It feels like seeing things for the first time through fresh eyes, understanding it is not your job to make anyone else happy. You are only responsible for your own happiness and will never again freely handover your power and identity again. Your journey starts now, as you start to rebuild a new life for yourself, you can create a new happy script this time considering and taking into account your feelings, wants and desires as a priority. Start to remind yourself daily of how valuable you are, begin to build up your self-esteem and confidence. Leave notelets around of positive affirmations which are visual reminders of your strength and worthiness.

I myself have a selection on my bedroom wall that I've turned into some art work, which are visual reminders each time I wake up in the morning of my ability to stay strong, stay positive and feel joy and gratitude for life. Again I have reminders of inspiring quotes on my fridge to reinforce warm positive nuggets of encouragement throughout the day. Start to focus and believe in yourself, anything is possible and you will start to experience around you a richer fuller diverse loving life, to appreciate and enjoy. Little by little you will grow stronger you will find your inner warrior. You will find your equilibrium, be at peace with who you truly are and those around you.

Your path may be long or it may be short and each individual persons journey will be different to the other, but I guarantee you it is a path worth taking out of the fog and into the light.

*Let your inner being guide you and trust that you will smile again, laugh again and find joy again.*

# EPILOGUE

This is not the end; this is just the beginning.

I hope that you can now see all is not lost, far from it.

Being woken up from under a Narcissist's spell is the start of realigning yourself to your true pure inner being.

Be fearless.

Stay strong and let this experience teach you a valuable life lesson.

Turn it into a positive opportunity for **Growth, Knowledge, self-empowerment** and **Freedom.**

*I believe in you, so start to believe in yourself!*

**'The cage is open so spread your wings and fly'**

Made in the USA
Middletown, DE
20 May 2019